Inclusion in the Early Years

Inclusion in the Early Years

Kay Mathieson

Open University Press

Open University Press
McGraw-Hill Education
McGraw-Hill House
Shoppenhangers Road
Maidenhead
Berkshire
England
SL6 2QL

email: enquiries@openup.co.uk
world wide web: www.openup.co.uk

and Two Penn Plaza, New York, NY 10121–2289, USA

First published 2015

A catalogue record of this book is available from the British Library

ISBN–13: 978-0-33-526270-0 (pb)
ISBN–10: 0-33-526270-8 (pb)
eISBN: 978-0-33-526271-7

Library of Congress Cataloging-in-Publication Data
CIP data applied for

Typesetting and e-book compilations
by RefineCatch Limited, Bungay, Suffolk

Printed and bound by CPI Group (UK) Ltd, Croydon, CR0 4YY

Praise for this book

"Kay Mathieson is a passionate advocate for making inclusive values the core of high quality early years practice so that every unique child can access their entitlement to support for learning and development. She starts with a fascinating journey through historico-political attitudes to special educational needs and disability. The contemporary case studies bring to life the joys, challenges and dilemmas involved for practitioners, children and parents. Their words alongside Kay's own reflections, knowledge and expertise make this a 'must-read' for all early years leaders and practitioners."

Helen Moylett, President of British Association of Early Education

Contents

Acknowledgements   ix
Introduction   xi

PART 1

The historical and political perspective   **1**

1   Shared beginnings: key legislation in the history of special educational needs and early years   3
2   The Warnock Report: a product of its time?   18
3   The legacy of the Warnock Report   29

PART 2

The enabling environment: what does success look like?   **47**

4   The role of the SENCO   49
5   EYFS: a principled approach   65
6   The Prime Areas of Learning in the EYFS and early identification of SEN   83

PART 3

Making the difference   **105**

7   The practitioner's perspective   107
8   The parents' perspective   122
9   The child's perspective   142
10   Looking to the future   158

Appendices   167
Bibliography   189
Index   201

Acknowledgements

The motivation and basis for this book have been my experience of working with many children, their parents and fellow professionals. Together they have taught me so much about recognizing and celebrating individual strengths and talents. Their inspirational approach to challenges and problem solving has been very humbling.

Particular thanks are due to those parents and colleagues who contributed case study material for the book. These include those from:

Brookhill Nursery School
Denehurst Day Nursery
Eastwood Nursery School and Centre for Children and Families
Modern Montessori International Croydon
Purley Nursery School
Ridgeway Primary School
Rowangate Primary School
Sure Steps Nursery
Telten Montessori Nursery School
Whytebeams Nursery School
Childminding Team, South Gloucestershire
Consultant Community Pediatrician, Milton Keynes

I would also like to thank these specific individuals who agreed to share their particular stories:

Claire, Irina, Louise, Annette, Julie, Emma, Becca, Caroline, Paula, Kelly, Joanna, Suzanne, Chinwe, Mami, Maxine, Frances, Noreen, Jade, Kelly, Anusha, Polijana, Muna, Adam, Nyani, George, Pam, Caron, Janice, Danielle, Julie, Vicky, and Ann. Thank you so much for your support.

No book is written by a single person, it is a process of collaboration, support and joint thinking. Some key individuals have made this process more manageable for me. The website, 'Education in England: the history of our schools', developed by Derek Gillard, has made access to original documents, including reports and parliamentary papers, a simple and straightforward process.

Ann Langston as series editor has helped me develop my thinking in shaping the key messages of the book. She has also improved the clarity of my writing and balance of the content through her thoughtful editing.

The journey of writing a book is often also a somewhat selfish one with hours spent tapping at the keyboard. Thank you, Simone, for all your support and encouragement – as always, I could not have done it without you.

Introduction

The Children and Families Act (2014) and the Special Educational Needs Code of Practice (DfE 2014a) open the next chapter in a long and arduous journey from educational segregation towards educational inclusion. It is timely to consider how far we have progressed and to reflect on the improvements to our practice that this Code of Practice can bring. This text sets out, firstly, to provide basic information about the political and historical context of early years and special educational needs in the UK, mainly focused on England. Secondly, the Early Years Foundation Stage Prime areas and characteristics of learning are explored as a key to understanding all children's development, but especially those with special educational needs. Thirdly, it offers a range of case studies to add to practitioners' own experiences of early years and special educational needs.

The three sections of the book are compiled with the intention of deepening our thinking about our own practice. Reflecting on our professional practice inevitably requires us to question our own personal beliefs, values and assumptions. The first section of the book offers some background to the possible origins of these, particularly in relation to disability. If our core beliefs, values and assumptions are aligned with the principles of the Early Years Foundation Stage, then the second part of the book will enhance and refine our thinking. Otherwise it will offer a pathway to look more closely at our understanding of children's strengths, learning and uniqueness. Finally, the third part of the book uses further case studies to provoke thinking about how our practice may be experienced by others. In reading and reflecting on the case studies, we can consider how to improve our personal, setting, team and sector practice.

A fundamental message is that in order to improve we need to truly engage and listen to those experiencing our professional practice. This includes children, parents, colleagues, other professionals and the local community. This engagement will begin with one interaction but build into a conversation that must continue through the challenging as well as the positive times. No effort is wasted; every setback is an opportunity to rethink.

The three agencies of health, education and social care are all charged with working more closely together. My experience is that in each of these services there are professionals 'on a mission' to make the systems and structures more flexible and responsive to those they seek to help. Every positive relationship with children, parents and colleagues contributes to a better experience for all and proves that when it works, the benefits are significant (Life Long Learning Programme 2010).

High quality provision

My professional journey has led me to believe that high quality early years practice has, at its core, inclusive values. The practitioners who demonstrate this in their everyday practice with all children and their families are inspirational. They demonstrate confident 'possibility thinking' about adapting routines, systems and approaches in order to be responsive to individual children and their families. There are no easy answers; however, the debate is no longer about segregation, integration or inclusion but about recognizing individual difference and striving to provide high quality provision for all. Only skilled practitioners who are intent on 'tuning into' all the children and parents will bring this about. The EYFS provides a structure for high quality provision, but the reality is that 'quality' is the gift of those working in the sector. The more informed, reflective and outward-looking we are, the more likely our practice will improve.

'Study the past if you would define the future' (Confucius)

In order to understand our current position it is useful to review the historical background that has led to the current early years landscape and attitudes of the twenty-first century. Increasing understanding of child development, including atypical development, has continued to inform our views in early years with special educational needs seen as 'normal development gone awry' (Herbert 2003: xiii). It is clear the journey of recognizing individual needs and increasing access to education has not always been smooth. The motives for change have been varied but the overall result has been more inclusion and recognition of competencies.

Recognizing and meeting children's needs

This is not, however, a time to be complacent. National statistics show that the number of children in England with statements of special educational needs has remained constant across recent years (2.8 per cent from 2008 to 2013). This, in an under-5s population (UK Census 2011: www.ons.gov.uk) that has increased by 406,000 since 2001. Notably only 0.6 per cent of children in maintained nursery provision have statements. This reflects the time taken from early identification through to statutory assessment. But when these statistics are combined with the fact that only about 50 per cent of children with disabilities attend maintained nursery provision, it also suggests the accessibility of settings and the success of 'early intervention' need further exploration.

Organization of the book

This book is presented in three sections; the first outlines some key histor-ical and political influences as a background to present-day provision. The second section considers the Early Years Foundation Stage (2014) and uses case studies to explore examples of effective practice. The third section, also based on case studies, gives an opportunity to consider early years provi-sion for children with special educational needs from the perspectives of children, parents and practitioners. Each section has three chapters that develop particular aspects or themes in more depth.

Part 1 *The historical and political perspective*

This section of the book explores some highlights in the UK legislative context. It gives an overview of the path to our current thinking about early education, who it is for and what it is trying to achieve.

Chapter 1 *Shared beginnings: key legislation in the history of special educational needs and early years*

The history of special educational needs and disability has some commonal-ity with the development of early years provision. Both have benefitted from research, medical and technological advances. This is not an exhaustive study but does outline some particular changes in policy direction in English history. This first chapter covers the late nineteenth and early twentieth centuries.

Chapter 2 *The Warnock Report: a product of its time?*

Chapter 2 looks at the major era of medical and technological advances in the late twentieth and early twenty-first centuries. Landmark reports such as that by Mary Warnock, exploring provision for children with special educational needs, encapsulated the thinking of the time and challenged common practice. This report revolutionized thinking and approaches to special educational needs in many ways. Although not perfect, much of it has stood the test of time, such as increased involvement of parents and children in decision-making and the development of a 'graduated response' to children's identified needs.

Chapter 3 *The legacy of the Warnock Report*

The political landscapes of the Blair era had specific influences on education as well as more general perceptions of family and society, as represented in the legislation of the time. The previous Thatcherite focus on individual responsibility and independence changed to the drive by Blair to tackle the impact of poverty and give every child a 'Sure Start' in life. These were powerful influences on both early years and special educational needs provision. We continue to work in a context of strong political influence so the final part of this chapter focuses on the future as informed by the Children and Families Act (2014).

Part 2 *The enabling environment: what does success look like?*

This second section explores the Early Years Foundation Stage statutory framework (2014) and its support of inclusive provision for all children. It considers the Early Years Transition and Special Educational Needs (EYTSEN) Project (Sammons et al. 2003), which followed around 3000 children from pre-school to the end of Year 1, which indicated the positive impact of attendance at high quality early years provision. This was shown to be particularly true for those at risk of having additional needs in cognitive and social domains of learning. However, the EYSTEN Project follow-up parental questionnaire identified that only 30 per cent of parents reported their child's needs had been identified during their pre-school experience. As a sector we have an important role to play in recognizing a child's particular needs and facilitating appropriate support. Early years practitioners are often on the front line, having conversations with parents about their child's existing or emerging needs. The way we discharge this responsibility will influence future attitudes and expectations of families in accessing help and support. Our attitude and knowledge of local pathways to support can provide both practical and emotional support for parents and carers.

Chapter 4 *The role of the SENCO*

A useful indicator of the quality of EYFS provision is the role the SENCO plays in leading practice as well as implementing the SEN support process. Sadly, in some settings little thought is given to the role or the potential the SENCO has to improve practice for all children. The SENCO's areas of expertise chime strongly with the principles of the EYFS:

- recognizing and meeting the needs of the Unique Child
- striving to develop positive relationships with children, parents, colleagues and those beyond the setting
- ensuring the emotional and physical environment is accessible and responsive to each child's needs
- using detailed observation, assessment and planning to offer opportunities that enhance learning

There is different terminology in the SEND Code of Practice (DfE 2014a), and there are still likely to be tensions in the SEN process but our common purpose remains to use our 'best endeavours' to meet each child's needs.

The SENCO also has to be proactive in seeking information, links and support beyond the setting. Engaging in the development of the Local Authority's 'local offer' and moderating decisions through SENCO networks offer professional development but also support continuous improvement.

'Providers must have arrangements in place to support children with SEN or disabilities' (DfE 2014a: 68). The case studies in this chapter explore a range of challenging situations and the SENCO role in implementing these internal processes while being mindful of external demands such as assessment timescales and transitions.

Chapter 5 *EYFS: a principled approach*

Case studies in this chapter explore the EYFS principles. First, they highlight the concept of the Unique Child as a clear inclusive message about recognizing each child's strengths, needs and differences. Second, it refers to 'positive relationships' leading to inclusion of family and special people in the child's life. This principle recognizes the importance of communicating together about the child's progress as demonstrated by practitioners with an inclusive attitude. Finally, the notion of an enabling environment is considered, particularly its accessibility, challenge and the opportunities it offers for facilitating each child's learning.

Five children are introduced, showing how working closely with parents can help overcome many barriers, for the benefit of not one child but all children. Jasmin and Mia were known to have special educational needs before attending their settings while for Andrew, Joshua and Roman, understanding of their needs was progressed through engagement with their early years provision.

Chapter 6 *The Prime Areas of Learning in the EYFS and early identification of SEN*

In this chapter we meet Darren whose specific needs were identified by conscientious practitioners in his day nursery. Based on a detailed case study, Darren's progress in the Prime Areas of Learning is considered. The designation 'Prime Areas of Learning' in the revised EYFS (2012 and 2014) focuses practitioners' thinking on personal, social and emotional development (PSED), communication and language (CL) and physical development (PD) as foundations for future learning. The implications for children needing additional support and the inter-relatedness of the three Prime Areas are examined with examples of effective practice.

Part 3 *Making the difference*

The chapters in Part 3 offer a selection of case studies demonstrating the real-life experience of inclusive early years practice. The case studies have been grouped together to communicate the perspectives of practitioners, parents and children. This allows the reader the opportunity to consider different viewpoints on the challenges and problem solving which are inherent in developing more effective inclusive approaches.

Chapter 7 *The practitioner's perspective*

This chapter begins with examples from the 'local offer' and the pathways linking early identification and early intervention. Practitioners share their thinking about successes, frustrations and suggestions related to their roles. Their accounts are also illustrative of the motivation and willingness of many to hold individual children and families' needs at the centre of their practice. While it is understood that no system is perfect, the role of individual practitioners in supporting parents is crucial to facilitating the most successful outcome for individual children.

Chapter 8 *The parents' perspective*

The Children and Families Act (2014) requires parents, children and young people to be central to decision-making related to their lives. In this chapter we are introduced to seven children, the first three, Steven, Josh and Hamsa, were identified as having additional needs while attending their early years provision. In contrast, Gordon's, Petra's, Hugo's and Anya's needs were recognized soon after birth. The case studies illuminate their parents' experiences of early identification and intervention in the EYFS. Their individual experiences are variable across geographical area, different services and individual practitioners. This variability gives rise to frustrations but also celebration and relief when individual practitioners listen carefully and work collaboratively with them. The examples of effective practice demonstrate how powerful the right support, delivered in the right way, at the right time can be. There are some very poignant stories that prompt reflection on our own individual practice. Having had the privilege of hearing these stories first hand, I feel frustrated at the lack of consistency and coherence of support that was available to families. On the other hand, it is inspirational to hear how individual practitioners, through their skill and insight are able to make services welcoming and accessible. Existing resources and approaches such as the Personal Child Health Record (the Red Book), Early Help, the Common Assessment Framework and the Team Around the Child are intended to support collaborative working but in the final analysis it is the quality of the relationships that leave families feeling supported, stronger and more confident.

Chapter 9 *The child's perspective*

This chapter illustrates how parents and practitioners have found ways to hear children's voices and incorporate this into their understanding. We focus again on Darren, Hugo and Anya and are introduced to Daniel. Ensuring children's views of their likes, dislikes and current interests informs our practice and is fundamental to high quality EYFS provision. This skilful pedagogy engages parents in their child's developing autonomy and view of the world. Through the challenges of recognizing a child's special educational needs, this level of understanding can also be of real emotional and practical support for parents.

Chapter 10 *Looking to the future*

The political landscape will continue to influence our professional and personal lives and in the early years, we have constant opportunities to make a positive difference to the experience of children and families. Perhaps bringing together what we have learned about supporting children with special educational needs can be harnessed more effectively to encourage a wider group of vulnerable learners.

Use of specific terminology

The phrase 'special educational needs' is generally used to reflect the current legislative context in the UK. In the historical section the wording and phrases of the time are used to illustrate how the terminology has changed over the years, reflecting different attitudes and understanding. A few children will enter EYFS settings with an Education, Health and Care Plan (formerly a Statement of Special Educational Needs) in place. However, the wider perspective of children whose support needs may become recognized while in early years provision must also be at the forefront of our thinking and practice. Both situations are, I believe, encompassed in the EYFS (2014) principle of the Unique Child and the requirement to recognize and meet each child's individual needs.

'Practitioner' is used to describe a trained professional regardless of which agency, i.e. health, education, social care, and irrespective of the level of qualification. 'Early Years Foundation Stage setting' and 'Early Years provision' are used as inclusive terms for the full range of types of provision, i.e. childminders, pre-schools, day nurseries, nursery classes, nursery schools and children's centres regardless of whether these are private, voluntary, independent or in the maintained sector. As all these types of provision are required to adhere to the Early Years Foundation Stage Statutory Framework, they will also 'have regard to' the Special Educational Needs Code of Practice and be subject to other relevant equalities and disability discrimination legislation.

'Parent' is used to include anyone with parental responsibility for a child such as birth, adoptive, foster and step-parents as well as carers and other family members fulfilling a parental role for a child.

Case studies

Parts 2 and 3 of the book feature a number of case studies – drawn from a range of early years provision – highlighting effective practice. In addition, parents' and practitioners' perspectives, collected through interview, illuminate differences in experience within and between families. The case studies illustrate the themes and topics under discussion in the book and offer profound insight to inform, support and improve individual and setting practice.

How to use this book

This book can be used in different ways for different purposes. To gain a deeper understanding of special educational needs and the wider issues involved in your thinking, it is important to explore Part 1 in depth, following up references where there are elements of interest or more information is needed. To challenge your own practice, develop your practical understanding or affirm your 'can do' approach, the case studies in Part 2 can be read separately. To build confidence that you can make a difference, Part 3 gives a wider context to your own experience by exploring different perspectives of special needs and support in early years provision. To challenge your thinking and reflect on your current practice through the parents', child's and practitioners' perspectives, reading all three chapters is advised.

The book raises and explores many aspects of early years practice in relation to special educational needs but the situation is continually evolving so the final chapter highlights how individual journeys can be influenced by both national and local policy as well as personal experience.

PART 1
The historical and political perspective

1 Shared beginnings: key legislation in the history of special educational needs and early years

Chapter themes

- The increased awareness of competition and relative academic performance internationally
- The influence of employment as a driver and outcome of education
- The two World Wars and their influences on attitudes and society

In 2014, the Children and Families Act took its place on the statute books with a SEND Code of Practice with a different tone and approach from its forerunner. In order to understand how this might impact on the experience of children with SEN and their families we need to recognize some of the influences that have brought us to this point. This chapter will outline some of the landmark legislation that has shaped the development of both early years provision and our understanding of, and attitude towards, the inclusion of all children in our settings. For a fuller exploration of historical perspectives, see also, Nutbrown, Clough and Selbie (2008), Farrell (2004), Armstrong and Squires (2012), and Norwich (2013).

As views in society change, medical and technological advances become commonplace and the political landscape develops, educational practice needs to evolve as a means of preparing our children adequately for their future lives. This is not an easy process, many individuals and groups have strong views about the relative importance of each aspect of education and the priorities for the learning and development of our young children. Our democratic political system in the UK offers a comprehensive process for gathering views and reviewing the details before legislation is finally enacted. In brief, the process is:

- concern raised about an element of our public life
- specialists assembled to gather evidence
- detailed report to inform legislation
- Green Paper draft of possible legislation for consultation
- White Paper further draft scrutinized by House of Commons and the House of Lords
- Bill of legislation formulated and further scrutinized
- Act receives Royal Assent (see www.parliament.co.uk for further details)

The political influences on our education system can be traced through the many Education Acts passed by the government. For example, Peel's Factory Act of 1802 requiring employers to provide instruction in basic reading, writing and arithmetic for apprentices. Also the Forster Act (1870) establishing 'elementary education' schools complementing those already provided by churches or private benefactors (Mackinnon et al. 1995: 46).

Education currently retains a high profile on the political agenda with both early years and special educational needs taking their turn in the spotlight. With the benefit of hindsight it is possible to see the highs and lows of their evolution. But, it is important to remember that none of the changes happened in isolation. International and global events brought about changes in focus or emphasis for our society and the education system needed to secure a positive future for our children.

It is commonly recognized that infants and those with special educational needs and disabilities have only recently been positively considered in the development of educational provision in the UK (Boyle and Topping 2012: 10). This has been mirrored in society generally, with some people with special educational needs and disabilities, previously being 'hidden away' and not viewed as active participants in our communities. Although younger children were not hidden away to the same extent, there was a strong sense of them being 'seen but not heard'. Education and health legislation are the two main categories explored, noting much cross-over and overlap as provision evolves for those with additional needs and disabilities.

The early twentieth century

Increasing awareness of competition in the international context

In 1902 the Balfour Act (HMSO 1902), controversial in its time, established mass schooling for both elementary and higher education levels in England, funded through taxation. The driver for this dramatic move was that 'continental' countries were judged to be more advanced than England and the impact on trade, industry and the economy was causing concern (Gillard 2011).

Specific concerns about the quality of the provision especially for younger children became a hotly debated topic. The Acland Report (HMSO 1908: 18) considered the pros and cons of attendance at school for children under the age of 5 years. At the time, such young children attended school only if their parents wished. However, medical and educational objections were raised indicating that the elementary schools were not an appropriate provision for infants.

In making their case, the Acland Committee stated the best provision was for young children to be at home with their mothers. The caveat, however, was that conditions in the home needed to be of a 'good standard'. Some homes and care arrangements were considered not to be sufficiently supportive of the children's mental and physical development. Evidence gathered by the committee showed a wide variation in conditions with some cases considered detrimental to the children's health. Considerable detail was included in the report of children's care. For example, evidence was presented of children looked after in their neighbourhood while their mothers were at work with some children drugged with laudanum, opium, gin or 'soothing syrup' in order to keep them docile and quiet. This concern led to the committee examining the most effective form of provision for children from these 'imperfect' home situations.

The committee was clear that any 'institution' for children of this age had to be appropriate in nature and of high quality. The influences of Jean-Jacques Rousseau, Johann Heinrich Pestalozzi, Friedrich Froebel, Rachel and Margaret McMillan and Maria Montessori are obvious in their conclusions (Nutbrown et al. 2010: 5). They indicated the premises should include:

- sufficient light, air and sunshine
- small furniture easily moved to allow 'games and play'
- flooring suitable for sitting comfortably and easy cleaning
- access to 'partly covered' outdoor areas with 'small plots for gardens
- facilities to give the children a bath if necessary

The 'curriculum' should:

- not restrict children's 'natural instinct for movement'
- have no rigid timetable
- not include formal lessons
- not include 'inspection or examination of results'

Ideally, children would spend half the day outside, including sleeping in the open air when tired. The quality of the teacher should be 'selected with scrupulous care', contrary to the then common practice that anybody was able to look after young children. The suggested staffing included assistants or nurses as well as teachers to support children. The influence of Friedrich

Froebel, a German educationalist who had been a student of Johann Heinrich Pestalozzi, is specifically mentioned, with his principles and training being the aspiration for high quality teaching (HMSO 1908: 23, 208).

Relative academic performance

The introduction of mass attendance at school in 1902 was not the success expected. The formal 'one-size-fits-all' approach, based mainly on rote learning with large class sizes, did not lead to all children making the same progress. Even an early form of 'performance-related pay' for teachers, linked to the attendance and attainment of pupils, did not result in success for all.

The Mental Deficiency Acts (1913–1938) mirrored the thinking of the time supporting segregation based on categorization, for example, using Intelligence Quotient (IQ) as a static measure of future individual mental capacity (HMSO 1913). Many science, health and education specialists were grappling with the current understanding about human beings, their similarities and striking differences. The lack of technology to explore the brains of the living, in particular, left talking and assessment of behaviour as the fundamental tools for research. The orientation of much research was focused on narrow definitions of being 'successful' and 'useful' in society; unsurprisingly a 'deficit' model was the norm. For example, the categories listed in the 1913 Act were 'imbeciles', 'idiots', 'feeble-minded' and 'moral defectives'. The definitions clearly articulate the deficit view that these individuals were lacking in some way and therefore considered unable to make a useful contribution to society.

The social expectations of the time also underpinned such categorizations. For example, the 'moral defective' label could be applied to unmarried mothers, based on an assumption that promiscuity, 'lack of moral fibre' and feeble-mindedness were linked so the women were admitted to asylums and mental hospitals (www.English Heritage.co.uk 2013).

The influence of war

Following the First World War, the 1926 Royal Commission on Lunacy and Mental Disorder (*British Journal of Nursing* 1926) took two years to review the evidence of the 'certification, detention and care of persons who were or alleged to be of unsound mind'. The commission's report recommended that the demarcation between mental and physical illness should be removed. It strongly suggested that a change of attitude in society was required, 'The keynote of the past has been detention; the keynote of the future should be prevention and treatment' (*British Journal of Nursing* 1926: 200).

The 1959 Mental Health Act (HMSO 1959) further changed the definition to 'mental disorder' including those with 'arrested or incomplete development of the mind'. This was still seen as demonstrating subnormal intelligence and related to the inability to lead an independent life. Significantly, the category of 'moral defective' was challenged by stating that this Act did not apply 'by reason only of promiscuity or other immoral conduct'. This represents a small but significant shift in thinking from the deficiency of the individual to acknowledging the role societal norms play in our judgements of those different to ourselves or the majority of the population.

The collective relief at the end of the war and the possibility of a brighter future contributed to a focus on creating a society providing positive opportunities for children, preparing them for healthy, useful lives. Children's early development was being considered from education, welfare, scientific and psychological perspectives. Around this time such key people as Friedrich Froebel, Rachel and Margaret McMillan, Rudolf Steiner, Maria Montessori, Melanie Klein and Susan Isaacs were focusing research on increasing understanding about early learning and development (Nutbrown 2010: 5). In 1923, the British Association of Early Childhood Education was established with Dr Susan Isaacs as its first president.

Following the First World War, children were gaining attention internationally too. The League of Nations adopted the Geneva Declaration of the Rights of the Child in 1924 (United Nations 1924) setting out aspirations for the world's children:

- The child must be given the means requisite for its normal development, both materially and spiritually.
- The child that is hungry must be fed; the child that is sick must be nursed; the child that is backward must be helped; the delinquent child must be reclaimed; and the orphan and the waif must be sheltered and succoured.
- The child must be the first to receive relief in times of distress.
- The child must be put in a position to earn a livelihood, and must be protected against every form of exploitation.
- The child must be brought up in the consciousness that its talents must be devoted to the service of its fellow men.

These aspirations chimed with the post-war focus on rebuilding economic and social stability in both the UK and Europe.

The Hadow Report 1931

The Hadow Committee explored in depth the current state of education for infants to adolescents. There were several reports published by the committee including reviews of curriculum for boys and girls, psychological testing, adolescent education, the use of books, and the structure of nursery, infant and primary schools.

The infant and nursery schools report commissioned by the Hadow Committee (HMSO 1933) documented the current thinking about:

- physical development (up to 7 years)
- mental development (up to 7 years)
- age limits and organization of the infant stage
- medical supervision, education and training of under-5s
- teaching and training of children in infant and nursery schools
- staffing
- premises and equipment

The sections related to young children's mental and emotional development were based on contributions from Dr Susan Isaacs. Knowledge of child development was increasing and the early years were newly recognized as having implications for later progress (HMSO 1933: 44).

The reference to children with special educational needs explained that (HMSO 1933: 94)

> We emphasise the importance of detecting early signs of retardation in children and of discovering the causes. We consider that separate classes or departments for retarded children in the infant stage are not necessary on educational grounds.
>
> (D. Gillard (2006) *The Hadow Reports: An introduction* www.educationengland.org.uk/articles/24hadow.htm)

The developing understanding of individual differences between children was also acknowledged – including the variation in typical growth patterns between boys and girls (HMSO 1933: 10). The likelihood that there might be similar variation in intellectual and emotional development was also raised. With this recognition came the desire for an educational system that was flexible and teachers who were adaptable in their approaches. The much quoted beginning of the Hadow Report gives a clear message about the committee's approach:

> At the heart of the educational process lies the child. No advances in policy, no acquisitions of new equipment have their desired effect unless they are in harmony with the nature of the child, unless they are fundamentally acceptable to him.
>
> (HMSO 1933: 9)

This much more positive view of individuals and their differences was in contrast to previous aspirations of conformity and everyone reaching similar levels of attainment.

Post-war priorities

Both World Wars influenced attitudes to, and the experiences of, people with a range of disabilities. Partly influenced by the return of war veterans in 1944 the Disabled Persons (Employment) Act came into being to 'make further and better provision for enabling persons handicapped by disablement to secure employment'. The economic pressures of the time also underpinned a view of education as a means to prepare as many citizens as possible for employment, including children with a range of disabilities (HMSO 1944: 2).

As part of the recovery programme, the Education Act 1944 (HMSO 1944a) set out a major restructure of education in England and Wales. This significant piece of legislation raised the importance of education in both national and local government. Nationally, the Ministry of Education was established and an Education Minister appointed. Locally, the duties and expectations of local education authorities were clarified. The Act focused mainly on primary, secondary and further education. However, local education authorities were required to 'have regard to the need for securing that provision is made for pupils who have not attained the age of 5 years' (1944 Education Act, Part II, para 8: 4). A similarly worded requirement related to provision for 'pupils suffering from any disability of mind or body'.

The regulations following the 1944 Education Act (Part II, para 33: 27) detailed local education authority responsibility to provide for children with disabilities by defining categories of pupils requiring 'special educational treatment'. These categories were:

- blind
- partially blind
- deaf
- partially deaf
- delicate
- diabetic
- educationally subnormal
- epileptic
- maladjusted
- physically handicapped
- speech defects

The provision for children with special educational needs and disabilities was seen as treatment not education and was determined by health professionals. Medical practitioners diagnosed disabilities and children were placed in specialist provision intended to cater for their needs. This provision was often geographically distant from the child's home and many were residential placements (Thane 2009: 1). Although medical practitioners made the diagnosis, it was the duty of the local education authority (LEA) to ascertain which children in their area were in need of special education. Parents could make a request for a medical assessment but could also be fined if they did not comply with the LEA request.

As well as education, the post-war UK government focused on welfare reform, resulting in the establishment of the National Health Service in 1946. Epidemics of poliomyelitis, tuberculosis and diphtheria resulted in large numbers of childhood deaths but also left many with lifelong disabilities. Before the establishment of the National Health Service the care and support of the children affected were mainly through charities. As a result, it was not uncommon for disabled children to resort to begging in the streets (www.nhs.uk).

Also in this period the National Foundation for Educational Research (NFER) began improving the quality of information and evidence available to inform educational policy and practice. Internationally too there was a shift in thinking about the role of education in society. The 1948 Universal Declaration of Human Rights now cited education as a right of every individual (United Nations 1948).

Interestingly at this time, nurseries and childminders were considered to provide health rather than educational provision. In 1948 the Nurseries and Childminders Regulation Act (HMSO 1948a) required registration with the local health authority and included a requirement to be inspected. During this period a range of provision for young children was established by churches, charities and philanthropists as well as the state health and education departments.

The mid-twentieth century

Understanding disability

Following the inception of the National Health Service, the development of paediatric facilities and hospital wards specifically for children began to emerge (http://www.nhs.uk/NHSEngland/thenhs/nhshistory/). In 1954 parents were, for the first time encouraged to visit their children, at least daily, during hospital stays. This change in policy was primarily based on new approaches by John Bowlby focused on understanding the importance of early attachment relationships. But it was also supported by paediatricians around the country who recognized the increased levels of stress and trauma experienced by hospitalized children as unnecessary and detrimental to their recovery (Birsch 2011: 9).

In 1958, another significant event impacted on society's response and understanding of disability and young children. A new drug prescribed for a range of ailments, but most notably to combat morning sickness in early pregnancy contained a chemical called thalidomide. It was found to have a dramatic effect on the early development of the foetus, typically affecting the growth patterns of limbs but also impacted on other internal organs. The total number of babies affected worldwide was thought to be around 10,000 (www.thalidomidesociety.org). The drug was withdrawn from circulation in the UK in 1961 and parents campaigned to raise awareness of the impact of thalidomide on children's lives. This challenged public thinking about disability, highlighting individuals who had been 'innocently' affected and the impact of disability on people's lives.

Developing early years provision

In 1962, the first national conference of the Association of Pre-school Playgroups (now known as the Pre-school Learning Alliance) was held in London. Local parents, predominantly mothers, were beginning to organize play-based sessional care for their children. The Association, concerned about establishing and maintaining the quality of provision, set up their own quality assurance process, making annual visits to monitor settings through the Approved Group Scheme. Being a member of this scheme also offered a range of support and training opportunities to learn about children's development (www.pre-school.org.uk).

The National Bureau for Cooperation in Childcare, later to become the National Children's Bureau, was established in 1963. Initially the focus of this charity was the plight of neglected children but it evolved to become the present multi-agency membership organization that campaigns to improve the lives of children (www.ncb.org.uk).

A significant medical development with long-term social implications took place in the early 1960s when the contraceptive pill became available. This was initially only prescribed for married women, by 1969 'the pill' was estimated to be taken by a million women. In 1967, the Abortion Act made abortion legal up to 28 weeks of pregnancy and reinvigorated the debates around when and if abortion was an acceptable course of action. When this was combined with the invention of (1956) and later (1970s) wide use of ultrasound scans (www.livescience.com) parents were put in a very different position when deciding to have a baby, and their expectations of the baby's health were changed in comparison with those of previous generations.

The Plowden Report

Education in the meantime was in need of another review, legislative change had been somewhat piecemeal in primary education since the Hadow Reports of the 1930s. So in 1967 the landmark Plowden Report provided detailed evidence of education in England and Wales. From the growing body of research and increased understanding of young children's development, a move towards a child- rather than a subject-centred curriculum evolved. In addition, the Plowden Report highlighted the role of the family and community in contributing to children's learning and development.

This 'new' child-centred approach saw the child as the starting point, with adults as facilitators of their increasing knowledge and understanding. This 'progressive education' built on the work of the pioneers recognized and still celebrated in early education such as Rousseau, Pestalozzi, Froebel and later Dewey, Montessori and Isaacs. In addition, Vygotsky's work became much more widely available around this time when his book *The Mind in Society* (1978) was translated into English from the original Russian text. The underlying belief in this progressive movement was that children should have the opportunity to learn through their play in a more egalitarian context than the previously hierarchical and elitist educational environment.

This fundamental change in the institution of education, particularly in England, was seen as revolutionary and threatening in some quarters. There was an opposing view based on the thinking that too much freedom was being given to children, and too little attention was being paid to discipline and the need to become a respectable member of society; this was fuelled by some high profile press reports about behaviour in specific primary schools (IOE 2009).

The Infant and Nursery Schools section of the Plowden Report revised the simplicity of the 'nature–nurture' debate, acknowledging the interaction between each child and their environment as determining outcomes for children. The concept of individual difference and variation is a fundamental message from Plowden that our education system needed to be flexible to accommodate a range of children's needs.

The conclusion of the committee was that:

> The picture of the growing child emerges as one in which each of a number of facets of physical, intellectual and emotional behaviour is developing slowly or fast, according to the individual and his circumstances.
>
> (HMSO 1967, Vol. 1: 19)

The puzzle at this time was the development of the brain and its role in learning ability. Some early experimental work with animals had indicated that there were 'sensitive or critical periods' in early brain development and function. However, it was not clear whether this was also true of human development. Clearly, the message was that until developmentally ready the child would be unable to assimilate specific concepts, understanding or skills.

The role of genetics was a little further understood than the development of the brain. The revelation that genes were not only active at birth but also influenced by hormones and chemicals in the womb and later the wider environment (HMSO 1967: 21) discredited some limiting judgements which had been made about children, for example, assessments of intelligence through Intelligence Quotient (IQ) testing (HMSO 1967: 26).

The report also made the connection between environmental and hereditary factors interacting and an overarching influence of socio-economic class. For example, family factors such as 'attitudes, traditions of child care, its child-centredness, its whole cultural outlook' were now brought into the mix. The impact of nutrition was also briefly mentioned as an underlying factor linking poverty with children's growth and development (HMSO 1967: 34).

A recommendation by the report that tried to combat this socio-economic disadvantage was the establishment of Educational Priority Areas. These areas were identified through a raft of data and criteria and were allocated additional funding. Aspects of provision such as improved teacher:pupil ratios, employing additional teaching assistants, building improvements, links with local teacher training facilities and social workers were expected to have a positive impact on the outcomes for children. The early experiences of children in these identified deprived areas were highlighted and a national expansion programme of nursery provision recommended. One advantage of this was the ready access that the School Health Services would have to enable early identification of difficulties and appropriate intervention.

The development of children's behaviour and the importance of emotions and nurturing relationships were seen as integral to the child's emerging identity. This was in stark contrast to earlier behaviourist approaches. Indeed, the Plowden Report highlighted that a 'major role' of the school was to help a child to come to understand their emotions rather than to suppress them. The interdependent influences of emotions, behaviour and learning were linked to the quality of the caring and nurturing relationships, not just at home but also in the community. The warning that a lack of this warmth and sensitivity in a child's early experiences was more likely to lead to 'maladjustment' than any 'illness in the child himself' represented a change in thinking. This began to establish behaviour as a means of communication rather than exclusively a premeditated deliberate action.

In the discussion about language development there emerged the most explicit reference to the need in school for 'compensatory opportunities'. This considered children whose language experience at home had been limited and so began their schooling at considerable disadvantage.

A theme also emerged regarding the need for further encouragement for parents to be involved in their children's schooling. The challenge was for schools to move beyond their direct influence on children to include parents, the intention being that this would support children's learning. Detailed suggestions of effective practice were included, such as parent–teacher meetings, parents associations, open days, reports for parents, and so on. There was also a suggestion that if parents did not attend these opportunities, then this should be followed up with a home visit at least once per year.

Nursery school provision

In response to the Hadow Report there had been an increase in privately run but grant-funded nursery schools. The Plowden Report highlights Rachel and Margaret McMillan as pioneers in this field. Nursery classes had also become a feature of some primary schools in England. There was a strong recommendation in the Plowden Report in favour of increasing provision for children under 5 (who were not subject to compulsory schooling under the 1944 Education Act). Nursery provision was seen as a 'good thing' not just for educational reasons but also to address concerns about young children's health, welfare and social development. However, it was acknowledged that expansion of nursery provision would be a significant financial investment at a time when budgets were already stretched.

The employment-driven social mobility characteristic of this era had resulted in family members being geographically further apart. This was noted by the committee as a lost opportunity for positive relationships with extended family. The increase in council housing needs being met through the construction of tall blocks of flats was, for obvious reasons, also seen as having the potential to negatively impact on children's social and outdoor play opportunities. Finally, the increase in married women going out to work and the isolation of those looking after their children at home were considered an additional strain on parenting capacity. It was now recognized that children would have to make a bigger emotional step from their immediate family relationships to having to deal with the social demands of the school environment.

Overall, nursery education was identified as a way of ameliorating some of the social and developmental risks to young children, not least identifying difficulties early so that help and support could be instigated. However, there was concern that children should not attend 'full-time' other than in exceptional circumstances so that attachment relationships at home with family, especially mothers, could be maintained. There was also mention of 'children's centres', envisaged as possibly combining provision for children from 3–5 years with 'day nurseries or clinics'. These establishments were to be under the supervision of a qualified teacher working with trained nursery assistants and with a minimum ratio of one adult to ten children.

Day nurseries at this time were still the responsibility of the Ministry of Health and were focused on 'relieving family problems'. The recommendation from Plowden was closer working between the health and education professionals. This confirmed the importance of emotional well-being and physical care but with increased emphasis on the child's educational progress. The suggestion was made that day nurseries could be seen as appropriate for children under 3 years of age while 3–5-year-olds would attend a more educationally orientated provision.

The Plowden Report acknowledged that there would always be a small number of children who would need specialist help (HMSO 1967: 296). This was in part the result of medical advances and improving living standards – meaning children were now surviving who would not previously have done so.

> When a disability is severe it is almost always recognized in early infancy ... Children with handicaps such as blindness, deafness, severe behaviour disturbance and the more severe forms of physical handicaps are usually sent to special schools, where appropriate equipment, small classes, and usually specially trained teachers are available to meet their particular needs.
>
> (HMSO 1967: 297)

Problems remained where children's less severe and harder to identify conditions led to debate and differing opinions about the most suitable educational provision. The committee reported that the weight of evidence from their witnesses was that whereever possible children should not be segregated but educated at their local school and in their local community. There was a strong recommendation for improved training for teachers and a greater understanding of the educational needs of individual children.

In 1968, the Summerfield Report explored the role of psychologists in education services. The Introduction sets out the early development of psychology and its role in developing our understanding of ourselves as human beings and more specifically the early development of young children (HMSO 1968: 3). The tenet of the Plowden Report echoes here with the focus on making the educational environment supportive and enabling for children's learning. The role of the psychologist was described as both preventative and remedial. The early identification of children's needs was seen as crucial in this process. Importantly, in the early years context the Summerfield Report raised the profile of the involvement of educational psychologists with children before compulsory school age.

In 1970, the first Act in the world to recognize the legal rights of people with disabilities was passed by the UK government (HMSO 1970). The Chronically Sick and Disabled Persons Act began to detail the responsibility of local authorities rather than health authorities to assess and provide appropriate services for those in their community with disabilities. This included assistance and adaptions at home, practical support with travel including holidays, access to recreational activities, appropriate education and public buildings. With the transfer of responsibility from health to education of providing for children with disabilities and the increasing understanding of individual learning, the stage was set for an in-depth consideration of provision for children with disabilities.

The 1970 Education (Handicapped Children) Act (HMSO 1970b) opened with a repeal of previous powers to deem a child as being 'unsuitable for education at school'. This set the benchmark that all children, regardless of their ability or disability, were to be considered as able to benefit from educational provision.

The group least mentioned in the legislation and committee reports were those who at this time were described as 'maladjusted'. In 1933, 'approved' schools had been established for children whose behaviour had led them through the courts. Although there was some general education available at these schools, the major focus was on social readjustment and a successful return to their local community.

Conclusion

This narrative, traced through the relevant legislation, indicates how scientific, medical, psychological, sociological and educational research has gradually influenced our collective understanding of child development and appropriate provision. The attitudes and motivations behind the interpretation and implementation of the legislation are less clear. Some would argue that the drive for every individual to contribute to the wealth and strength of the community led to the segregation and categorization of individuals to enable them to be used as 'factory fodder'. Others would lend weight to the thinking prevalent in the eugenics movement of the 1940s that those categorized as defective would reduce the strength of the general population. These are all contentious views. This book does not seek to explore them in great depth but to raise awareness of the historical context that sets the scene for current thinking. The priorities of our society, and the way in which individuals, regardless of their skills and abilities, are influential continue to evolve. However, our own individual perspectives contribute to the society norms and it is important that those working with young children are conscious of these influences.

The Plowden Committee stated:

> The school must provide for and cherish all its members. Some handicaps evoke more sympathy than others. Blindness, for instance, excites almost universal sympathy, deafness much less, while maladjustment is often exasperating, and certain kinds of physical deformity are felt by many to be repellent.
>
> (HMSO 1970a or 1967: 300)

Although the specific language may have changed, the six recommendations in the Plowden Report are still something we strive for today.

1   Early identification from birth onwards
2   Professionals working together to facilitate continuous assessment
3   Counselling support for parents of children with 'handicaps'
4   Detailed assessment to inform appropriate provision
5   Changes in labels and language to decrease stigma
6   More appropriate training for teachers

This may be taken as evidence of the aspirational nature of the work of the Plowden Committee or as testament to the frustratingly slow progress of reform.

Key Points

- The UK journey from segregation towards inclusion has been brought about by increasing knowledge and understanding in science, health and education supported by key groups campaigning for equality
- Significant events such as wars and epidemics can be powerful agents of change in social attitude, bringing as they do medical and technological advances alongside changed experiences such as increased awareness of disability and its implications for individual lives
- Diverse political and philosophical perspectives on the 'purpose' of early years education, its relation to future employment and the UK place in international economies create varying tensions in the system

2 The Warnock Report: a product of its time?

Chapter themes

- The impact of increasing knowledge and understanding of special educational needs and disabilities on inclusive approaches in education
- Recognizing an individual's potential for learning and contributing to society
- The possibility of an inclusive society

The knitting together of events in the previous chapter demonstrates how these fuelled progress in many areas of science, psychology and medical advances. But also how attitudes in society can be influenced, evolving and gradually changing over time. The political process and the associated documents give a sense of the time but do not give an exhaustive picture of an individual's experience. Therefore there would, as today, have been examples of exemplary practice existing alongside low quality, uninformed practice. The pattern of the legislative process is to gather information from research and advances in understanding and to compare this with current practice. The purpose of the legislation is to improve practice to the quality of the best and make this as widespread as possible. In essence, the narrative illustrates how we have, and still are, gradually learning more about ourselves as human beings and how we strive to improve the future for our children.

This chapter considers some of the legislation that influenced the period from 1974 to 1995. As the picture unfolds we can understand more coherently the current provision of caring for and providing education for all our younger children.

The Warnock Report took four years to review provision for children with a range of 'handicaps' (HMSO 1978: 8). The committee looked in depth at the medical, social and educational needs of those in education with special educational needs and disabilities. The work was distributed between four sub-committees divided as follows;

1   Children under 5
2   Children with handicaps in ordinary schools
3   Day special schools and boarding provision
4   School leavers and their needs

Smaller working groups focused on other specific aspects such as:

- Curriculum
- Confidentiality and the flow of information
- Advice and support in special education
- Coordination of services
- Special Education Forms procedure
- Research and development

In the course of their investigations the committee members also undertook international visits to gather information about alternative approaches to supporting children with special educational needs.

Moving from a 'deficit' view

The committee identified two specific purposes of education for children with 'handicaps': first, 'to enlarge knowledge, experience and imaginative understanding' which they recognized as underpinning awareness of moral values and capacity for enjoyment; second, to be an 'active participant' and 'responsible contributor' to society achieving as much independence as possible on leaving formal education. These goals were the same for children without 'handicaps' but it was understood that there would be greater variation in their achievement and the amount of help needed to reach the goals. This approach is a significant change in thinking from previous legislation where the identification of difference and 'deficit' was a trigger for a 'treatment' paradigm. Further, the committee emphasized a wider view of learning, seeing parents as important educators and stating that all adults involved with the child should be working together.

The purpose of education

The development of medical science and improved living standards had resulted in many children surviving who would not previously have lived beyond infancy. The implications were not lost on the committee who in their report outlined their belief that while some may question whether these children should be educated at all, they were clear that:

> education, as we conceive it, is a good, and a specifically human good, to which all human beings are entitled. There exists, therefore, a clear obligation to educate the most severely disabled for no other reason than that they are human. No civilized society can be content just to look after these children.
>
> (HMSO 1978: 6)

The radical combination of having common goals for all children and seeing education as an entitlement for everyone as of human right was quite a different language and perspective from previous reports and legislation.

Towards inclusion: new thinking, new words

Further, the conceptualization of special educational needs as a 'continuum' built a strong bridge linking those previously considered 'normal' and 'abnormal'. This challenged the public to accept that the range and diversity of ability and need were progressed by talking less of 'handicaps' and more about the level of help required. This was furthered by changing the now outdated language of 'handicap' to special educational needs and disabilities.

Extending the capacity of mainstream schools to include children with special educational needs was a challenge. But the end of selection for secondary schooling in the 1960s encouraged the development of 'remedial' approaches to education for those who were not making expected progress. The 'integration' of children with special educational needs became the focus of attention.

Integration was initially seen as the opposite of the previous regime of segregation. However, individual cases highlighted the stark difference between children being in the same room as their mainstream peers and, those fortunate enough to be socially accepted as well as having their learning needs met. With the focus on support needs came a growing understanding that for some children early support could in fact lessen the level of support needed in the future.

Early intervention

This concept of early intervention was developed through several programmes still evident today such as Portage. The Portage Home Visiting

Service was introduced to the UK in 1975. This approach came from the town of Portage in Wisconsin and was specifically designed to support children with special educational needs. The programme involved a specially trained worker visiting the child's home on a regular basis, usually weekly, engaging the child and parent in play activities to support the child's learning and development.

Labelling, categorizing and early identification

Estimating the numbers of children likely to be included in the new broader concept of 'special educational needs' was difficult to ascertain since previous research had used a range of different criteria. However, the Warnock Committee estimated from the information available that approximately 17 per cent of children were likely to have special educational needs. Further, they differentiated between long- and short-term needs and, taking this into account raised their expectation to 20 per cent of children having a special educational need 'at some point in their school career'.

Three types of special educational needs were identified:

1   Special equipment, resources, modified environment and specialist teaching techniques
2   Special or modified curriculum
3   Modification to the social structure and emotional climate

Considerable explanation was given about the pros and cons of categorization and its incumbent labelling of children. The committee highlighted the reality of the experience of children whose lives had been blighted by such labels and the associated social stigma.

This led them to suggest more general descriptive terms that might be helpful but not stigmatizing, such as 'learning difficulties', which could be mild, moderate or severe. Continued monitoring of numbers of children with special educational needs to plan appropriate provision was still needed, however, so criteria were suggested. The criteria categorized the form of provision that would best meet the child's special educational needs such as access to:

- teachers, on either a full- or part-time basis, with appropriate qualifications or substantial experience or both
- other professionals, on either a full- or part-time basis, with appropriate training
- an educational and physical environment with the necessary aids, equipment and resources

It was hoped this would finally remove the idea of 'treatment' for children and replace it with a more helpful approach.

Although the Warnock Committee focused on the group of children most likely to access mainstream schooling with some additional help, they recognized that this was not the full picture. Their statistical evidence suggested that there would remain approximately 2 per cent of the child population who would need specialist provision. In order to secure this the committee recommended a statement of special educational needs requiring local authorities to undertake a multi-professional assessment to clarify the child's needs and appropriate provision.

The role of Health Visitors and access to relevant information between health and education services was extensively considered in the Warnock Report. Notwithstanding the issue of confidentiality, information sharing was recognized as crucial. The assessment of children's special educational needs was envisaged as a five-stage process. This was intended to establish a practical way to sustain the idea of a continuum of need and provision. Whatever the outcome, it was recommended that progress and effectiveness of specialist support should be reviewed, at least on an annual basis but more frequently when transitions were about to take place. The issue of children whose first language was not English was also addressed, requiring at least one of those carrying out the assessments to speak the child's first language. The cultural bias of assessment procedures was challenged, due to the disproportionate representation of West Indian children in specialist provision. For children for whom a diagnosis was likely, there were further difficulties as witnesses presented to the committee examples of poor practice and lack of support. The practical and emotional issues for parents when hearing about the discovery of their child's special educational needs were considered at length. The evidence gathered by the committee suggested that parents were not well supported by professionals at this crucial time. The need for sensitivity, but also practical support, was emphasized including the possibility of the parent inviting another professional, a 'Named Person', to be present to ask relevant questions and gather salient information.

The disability rights movement

From the 1970s the experiences of people with disabilities gained a higher profile as the disability movement and the demand for equality won support. Around this time organizations such as the Union of the Physically Impaired Against Segregation (UPIAS), the British Council of Disabled People's Organisations (BCODP) and the Alliance for Inclusive Education (ALLFIE) were instrumental in bringing together different groups with common aims. The core change that these organizations brought about was that they were run 'by people with disabilities for people with disabilities'. In contrast to the historic ethos of being 'done to', this represented a milestone in hearing the real voices of people with disabilities and their opportunity to articulate their own argument for changes in society (Alliance for Inclusive Education 2013).

The development of the internet in the 1990s enabled the 'information revolution' of the World Wide Web (www.internetsociety.org). The internet, along with television, supported the communication links between disability action groups strengthening the sense of belonging to a large increasingly influential group. In contrast to the segregated, specialist experiences of their younger lives, many adults with disabilities and special educational needs were empowered to strive for equality and choice not just in education but also daily living.

Comparison and collaboration

The Organisation for Economic Co-operation and Development (OECD) came into being in 1961 and saw the need for collaboration between countries in order to identify and address common problems. In 1988, the OECD launched a project, Indicators of Education Systems (INES) to enable consistent indicators to be used for international comparison (www.oecd.org). One result of this work was moving from comparing participation in education to testing and assessment of impact. Similar thinking is demonstrated in the 1988 Education Reform Act (HMSO 1988) which radically changed the structure of education, introducing the National Curriculum and associated assessments for children in compulsory schooling. The expressed purpose of this legislation was to raise standards of attainment and make schools more accountable for the progress of their pupils. Further, this Act introduced delegation of finances to schools and established 'grant-maintained schools'.

Individual needs

The focus on individual children's needs is evident in the 1989 Children's Act (HMSO 1989) that charged courts with keeping children's welfare as a 'paramount consideration'. The courts were expected to ascertain the child's own views wherever possible to inform proceedings. Further, each local authority was required to provide registered day care for 'children in need' until they were 5 years old or not attending school in their area. This included provision for 'supervised' activities outside of school hours and in the holidays. Local authorities inspected this provision at least annually, inspectors were able to enter day care or childminding premises 'at any reasonable time'.

This Act in the context of 'children in need' also required the local authority to maintain a register of children with disabilities in their area. In addition, they had to provide services that minimized the effect of their disabilities, and gave children the 'opportunity to lead lives which are as normal as possible'.

The developing thinking of meeting children's social, educational as well as medical needs was not just a focus in the UK as the Convention on the Rights of the Child in 1990 (UNICEF 1990) shows. The 54 Articles of the Convention set out the protection for children to be provided through the laws and actions of the relevant government in each country. UNESCO (United Nations Educational, Scientific and Cultural Organisation), UNDP (United Nations Development Programme), UNFPA (United Nations Population Fund), UNICEF (United Nations Children's Fund) and the World Bank also came together in the Education for All movement adding further support.

Consistency and coherence

However, as local authorities developed provision in the UK, it was increasingly becoming a system based on chance. In 1990, the Rumbold Report, *Starting with Quality* (HMSO 1990) reviewed the educational experiences offered to 3- and 4-year-olds. Although the remit for the report was focused on the quality of early years provision, there were also concerns raised about the lack of availability of provision. At this time the nature of early years provision included:

- local authority nursery schools and classes
- reception classes
- playgroups
- pre-school playgroup associations

This report opened up the idea that all those who were involved with young children contributed to their learning, not just teachers and parents; this included childminders, nannies, playgroup workers, nursery nurses and practitioners in day nurseries. At this time it was estimated that around 10 per cent of children started compulsory schooling without any previous experience of childcare or pre-school provision. The role of parents was still highlighted as crucial and early years educators were seen as instrumental in building parental confidence and supporting their children.

The trend at this time was for increasing numbers of 4-year-olds to be accepted into school reception classes, mainly driven by falling primary school rolls. However, the quality of this provision was judged to be variable and concerns were raised about the appropriateness of the equipment and learning experiences offered.

A focus on the early years

The Rumbold Report (HMSO 1990) recognized early years as a period of rapid growth, reiterating the importance of individual difference and noting recognizable patterns in development. For the 10 per cent of children who did not have access to pre-school provision, this variation would be even greater. Characteristics such as exploring, being active learners and making sense of the world through meaningful play experiences were valued.

> Play is a powerful motivator, encouraging children to be creative and to develop their ideas and test out what they know and can do.
>
> (HMSO 1990: 7)

The adults working with children were fundamental to nurturing this play, so that 'With encouragement and stimulation, this curiosity will develop into a thirst for, and enjoyment of, learning.' This needed to happen in the context of close positive relationships with parents and adults at home. A strong statement was included rejecting the idea that there should be a 'curriculum' of any kind for these young children. Rather, a flexible framework, underpinned by clear principles should be provided to guide practitioners in meeting children's varying needs. This framework would assist practitioners to avoid over-formalizing the learning opportunities for the young children in their care. An HMI Report (HMSO 1989a) had also highlighted that:

> Play that is well planned and pleasurable helps children to think, to increase their understanding and to improve their language compet-ence. It allows children to be creative, to explore and investigate materials, to experiment and to draw and test their conclusions . . . Such experience is important in catching and sustaining children's interests and motivating their learning as individuals and in co-operation with others.
>
> (HMSO 1990: 11)

Improving quality

The concept of 'self-monitoring' was advocated for those providing educa-tional provision for young children in order to continually improve the quality of the children's experience and the adults' professionalism. The investment in 'non-contact' time for adults to engage more effectively with parents was an important development in practice.

The idea of 'continuity and progression' for children emphasized in the Education Reform Act (HMSO 1988) now gave rise to concern that there would be pressure on ensuring children had reached the required standards ready for compulsory schooling, rather than enabling their individual development. The language of observation, planning and assessment emerged as the rigorous means of ensuring appropriate learning opportunities for young children and monitoring their progress over time.

Inclusion: an international agenda

The UNESCO World Conference on special needs education in 1994 was held in Salamanca, Spain, with representation from 92 governments and 25 international organizations. The fundamental objective was to promote inclusive education, the ideal of education for all children. The conference took a wide definition of inclusion and a stated conviction that improving the effectiveness of provision for those who were vulnerable would have a positive impact for others too (UNESCO 1994).

The delegates signed up to the following beliefs that:

- Every child has a fundamental right to education, and must be given the opportunity to achieve and maintain an acceptable level of learning.
- Every child has unique characteristics, interests, abilities and learning needs.
- Education systems should be designed and educational programmes implemented to take into account the wide diversity of these characteristics and needs.
- Those with special educational needs must have access to regular schools which should accommodate them within a child-centred pedagogy capable of meeting these needs.
- Regular schools with this inclusive orientation are the most effective means of combating discriminatory attitudes, creating welcoming communities, building an inclusive society and achieving education for all; moreover, they provide an effective education to the majority of children and improve efficiency and ultimately the cost-effectiveness of the entire education system.

The Salamanca Statement justifies child-centred pedagogy because this approach recognizes that human differences are normal. Consequently, it is the learning which must be adapted, rather than fitting the child into rigid approaches. The early identification of a child's individual needs, leading to appropriate learning opportunities that supported their 'physical, intellectual and social development and school readiness' were seen as the core of the successful inclusive provision. It was believed this should be integrated with health and care needs in order to support the individual's holistic development.

Life after Warnock

The quality of education provision continued to be an issue and a more cohesive approach to inspection was seen as the answer. The 1992 Education Act (Schools) (HMSO 1992) established the Office for Standards in Education (Ofsted) with the power to inspect schools, including nursery schools. Concerns about the financial implications of meeting all children's needs and whose financial responsibility: school, local authority or central government, it was to meet the costs, were ongoing.

In addition to introducing the 'Grant Maintained School' with increased independence from the local authority, the Education Act (1993) established a Special Educational Needs Code of Practice, as guidance for practitioners. The definitions for special educational needs from Warnock were maintained (HMSO 1993: 101). The expectation that children should be educated at their local mainstream school was reinforced so long as this ensured:

- the child received provision which was required by his special educational needs
- the education of other children was not compromised
- this was an efficient use of resources

(HMSO 1993: 100)

Beyond the educational arena, society was being encouraged to change its thinking and more importantly its attitudes. Disability rights campaign groups had an increasingly strong voice and influence on policy, as seen in the Disability Discrimination Act 1995 (HMSO 1995). Finally, some of the barriers to employment and accessibility of services for those with disabilities were being recognized and addressed. The Act established this definition:

> A person has a disability if he has a physical or mental impairment which has a substantial and long-term adverse effect on his ability to carry out normal day-to-day activities.

(HMSO 1995: 1)

Access to premises, particularly public buildings and specifically schools, was a key issue and it was felt that progress was not fast enough. The Act required those providing goods and services not to treat those with disabilities 'less favourably than others'. Local authorities and schools had to develop accessibility plans to clarify the progress they were making in developing accessible provision.

Conclusion

This chapter has reviewed some milestones in the evolution of our education system, including reference to the purpose of education itself alongside new language about rights and entitlement to education. The tensions between provision for the majority of children and meeting the needs of the minority were heightened by the development of an international comparison of the effectiveness of educational systems.

The Warnock Report revolutionized general thinking about disabilities and the inclusion of those with special educational needs in mainstream educational provision. There was also renewed interest in early years, considering both the quality and quantity of provision nationally. This focus on the youngest children raised awareness of the efficacy of offering support early in a child's life to reduce the need for later support. These emerging themes are now very familiar in professional discourse about early years and special educational needs. The challenge remains, however, for consistent high quality provision with confident practitioners who take account of individual children's needs.

Key Points

- The Warnock Report resulted in a significant shift in emphasis from segregation to inclusion, and introduced the idea of a 'graduated response' underlining that special educational needs are not always permanent, and that early intervention can lessen future levels of need
- The disability rights movement, in bringing together disparate groups to focus on a common purpose, dramatically raised awareness of their experiences and issues of equality of opportunity, access and autonomy in their lives
- Consistency and coherence of high quality provision for early years and special educational needs rely on individual practitioners, local support with monitoring and central legislation, all working towards a common purpose

3   The legacy of the Warnock Report

Chapter themes

- Many children's needs are often recognized too late to enable effective support

- Families' and children's voices should be heard and be central to decision-making

- There is continued need for greater collaboration between services and multi-agency working

Previous chapters have outlined the changes to early years and special educational needs provision which has haltingly brought us to the twenty-first century. Entrenched difficulties of agencies not working together, not having common aims or supporting consistent quality, continued to dilute the intentions of legislation. It also frustrated the campaigners, whether their focus was special educational needs or early years. The government's allocation of funding became a matter of public debate as information was more accessible and campaigners rallied support to influence politicians' views. Education became the topic of the day and a political priority to improve rankings in an increasingly competitive labour market. Mostly this was a response to the particularly high unemployment figures of the early 1980s (www.ons.gov.uk). The impact of unemployment and low wages on household income was beginning to be linked with children's early experiences and poverty was recognized as a risk factor in young children's development.

Extending early years provision

Seeing early years provision as a potential protective factor for young children is central in the 1996 Nursery Education and Grant Maintained Schools Act (HMSO 1996). This Act defined nursery education as 'that which was provided for children prior to the term before their fifth birthday'. A voucher system was introduced to enable parents to choose where their child received their nursery provision. The expressed intention was to make government-funded nursery provision available to all 4-year-olds. Questions began to be asked about whether current reception classes in schools were appropriate provision for 4-year-olds. The inspection process of the time gave no guarantee that those inspecting early years provision in schools would have appropriate experience. As a result, this Act required the Office for Standards in Education (Ofsted) to enlist appropriately qualified nursery school inspectors.

What was the purpose of early education?

Following 18 years of Conservative government, 1997 saw a Labour government returned for the following 13 years. The Labour Party had set out its plans for education in its 1994 document, *Opening Doors to a Learning Society* (Labour Party 1994). The government identified the twenty-first century as one full of possibilities with education its first priority. There was a promise to invest in early years provision, increase availability of nursery education, and raise the professional status of those working in the sector. This approach was based on a raft of evidence that investment in high quality early years provision could lead to reduced expenditure in the longer term as children's educational outcomes and inclusion in society would be improved. The 1997 White Paper *Excellence in Schools* (HMSO 1997) set out the details of the Labour Party's education agenda and what the new government hoped to achieve. From 1998 there followed documents and policy initiatives in unprecedented quantity, designed to bring about consistent improvement and access to the education system.

The impact of poverty on children's learning and achievement was acknowledged as a significant barrier. The intention was to 'overcome economic and social disadvantage and to make equality of opportunity a reality' (HMSO 1997: 3). This included tackling intergenerational disadvantage and disaffection. To positively impact on such long-standing difficulties no one individual or agency could bring about the desired change. The joint efforts of all, parents as well as, professionals from health, education and social care engaging in a common purpose was needed. High quality early years provision became available for all 4-year-olds, whose parents wanted it.

Standards were to be raised with a focus on literacy and numeracy in schools, with national guidelines devised and implemented to support best practice. Targets and performance monitoring were used to compare schools' impact on pupils' achievements. A national team of advisers began to train and work with local authorities raising the quality of teaching literacy and numeracy in schools. Training that developed skills of differentiation and personalizing learning was a priority.

Inspiration also came from the USA, in the form of the Headstart programme. It had begun as a pilot in 1965, designed to tackle the effects of poverty on young children's learning, health and well-being and was showing promising results. The research design and data collection from this programme were comprehensive, based on five specific objectives:

- Enhancing healthy growth and development
- Strengthening families as the primary nurturers of their children
- Providing children with educational, health and nutritional services
- Linking children and families to needed community services
- Ensuring well-managed programs that involve parents in decision-making

(Headstart Program Performance Measures, Second Progress Report 1998, available at www.acf.hhs.gov)

The positive impact of early years provision was accepted and the focus on giving children a 'headstart' in their learning gained momentum. The School Curriculum and Assessment Authority had published minimum standards or 'desirable learning outcomes' for young children as a step towards the now established National Curriculum (DfE 1999). Schools were to assess children's learning when they first attended school in order to monitor the progress over time. With more flexible teaching it was hoped this approach would encourage challenging learning opportunities but also offer support when appropriate.

Community of learners?

Following the model of Education Action Zones, established in areas of social and economic deprivation, schools were expected to work together meeting the needs of their local community of learners. Parents, as previously, were recognized as a 'child's first and enduring teachers', with family learning seen as a way of improving the skills of adults as well as children. This included basic skills and supporting positive approaches to parenting. Building on the Family Literacy initiative, devised by the Department for Education and Employment (DfEE) and the Basic Skills Agency in 1993, including grandparents and extended family members, to try to tackle the intergenerational socio-economic disaffection with education.

The use of ICT and the internet to support learning was high on the agenda and the National Grid for Learning was set up to enable collaborative working between staff, pupils, schools and communities. Data about pupil outcomes was scrutinized as evidence of school effectiveness and contributed to the increasing accountability of schools. Schools, however, argued that the simplistic data did not take account of the difficult circumstances in which some of them were working. Consequently, the opportunity to use such information as evidence of school failure as well as success was recognized as potentially very divisive.

'Excellence for all children'

The themes of inclusion, learning for all, and entitlement to high quality educational provision were central to the 1997 Green Paper, *Excellence for All Children: Meeting Special Educational Needs* which was produced with the National Advisory Group on SEN (DfEE 1997). This document challenged previous approaches to special educational needs and promoted inclusion in local mainstream provision. The intended outcome was to be more consistency in provision, earlier identification and intervention to support children's learning needs.

The 1994 SEND Code of Practice had embedded tensions by giving local education authorities responsibility for identifying and meeting children's special educational needs, but also giving them the role of controlling access to specialist provision (Dyson et al. 2002: vi). As a result the Statement of Special Educational Needs process had become an unwieldy and bureaucratic system increasingly leading to battles between parents and local education authorities. The contentious issue was not recognizing the child's needs but how these needs could be met. Parents consistently articulated strong views about the quality of provision, the expertise of the staff and whether they wanted their child educated in a mainstream or special school environment. Local authorities were very conscious of the financial implications, not just for placement but also for providing transport to and from schools. So it was hoped that the focus on inclusion in mainstream provision, set out in the Green Paper (DfEE 1997) would ease this tension. Further, it was hoped that the focus on meeting children's individual learning needs would also have a positive impact on the quality of teaching and learning for all children.

Local partnership working

Major reforms in the 1998 Education Act (HMSO 1998) defined a new approach. The engagement of local parents as well as the private, voluntary and independent sector in developing provision for young children and families was ensured through direct funding streams linked to specific targets. Local representative forums, known as Early Years Development and Childcare Partnerships (EYDCPs), had to oversee development of local early years and childcare provision.

Underpinning this expansion and improvement in the early years sector was an expectation that all provision would be inclusive and accessible for children with special educational needs. Teams of Area SENCOs (Special Educational Needs Coordinators) were established in each LA to support EYFS settings

With this strong central direction, change happened rapidly, particularly as funding streams were 'ring fenced' restricting local authorities from diverting resources elsewhere.

Early years provision was at last coming under the spotlight and there were many campaigners, academics and experts waiting in the wings to optimize the opportunity. Concerns about the variability in quality of provision were tackled with the production of the Curriculum Guidance for the Foundation Stage published in 2000 (QCA 2000). Although there was controversy about the concept of a 'curriculum' for our youngest children, that is for 3- to 5-year-olds, the guidance clarified expectations, emphasizing support for the individual child to progress in their learning and development.

Special educational needs and disabilities

Equality of opportunity emerged as a central pillar of disability rights campaigns, strongly influencing the 2001 Special Educational Needs and Disability Act 2001 (SENDA) (HMSO 2001). This Act required that a person with disability should not be treated less favourably than a non-disabled person. Unlike previously, this legislation was 'anticipatory' requiring those responsible for services, as well as buildings, to plan for and continually improve accessibility. This included early years providers, whether private, voluntary, independent or maintained, and took account of parents with disabilities as well as children.

The Special Educational Needs Code of Practice (2001), following SENDA, explicitly promoted inclusion in mainstream schools for children with disabilities. Exceptions to this were where it was contrary to the wishes of parents or, it adversely affected education for other children.

Children in early years had a significantly higher profile in this document than previously with the graduated response being described as Early Years Action and Early Years Action Plus in parallel with the school process. Intervention was defined as action which was 'additional to or different from' that offered for the majority of children. Individual Education Plans (IEPs) were to be used more effectively to define specific targets for learning, evidence rate of progress and measure the effectiveness of support provided. However, contrary to the spirit of the Code of Practice (2001), IEPs, disappointingly in some cases, became a criterion for progressing towards statutory assessment and specialist placement rather than meeting children's specific needs. Tight timescales for submitting applications to local authorities for statutory assessment, often a 'passport' to specialist provision, became the driver for producing IEPs and demonstrating lack of progress and high need, so making the case for increased support.

The Care Standards Act 2000 informed by the National Care Standards Commission (HMSO 2000) set out the minimum standards for a range of provision for children including day care and out-of-school provision. This took forward some of the promises from the 1997 *Excellence in Schools* White Paper (HMSO 1997), as did the Education Act 2002 (HMSO 2002) which stated that as a society we had to improve the opportunities for children beyond the previously accepted school day. The development of after school, breakfast and holiday clubs created childcare facilities often from eight to six o'clock each day. However, some geographical areas were served better than others and issues of quality of provision were a constant concern.

How early is early?

With the success of the Curriculum Guidance for the Foundation Stage which brought together principles and approaches for children from 3 to 5, the need for similar guidance for younger children was recognized. *Birth to Three Matters* (DfES 2003a) was published not as a 'curriculum' but information and guidance for practitioners. This guidance brought together private, voluntary and maintained sector provision with a common set of principles and focused on four aspects of children's development described as:

1 A strong child
2 A skilful communicator
3 A competent learner
4 A healthy child

Birth to Three Matters was an inclusive document championing all children as 'competent learners' from birth and guiding practitioners to work closely with parents to recognize children's learning and development through their play. This guidance emphasized these earliest years as important in their own right and not merely preparation for later learning. In 2007, *Birth to Three Matters* combined with the Curriculum Guidance for the Foundation Stage to form the Early Years Foundation Stage framework (DfES 2007). This provided statutory guidance for all early years provision, private, voluntary, independent and maintained sector for children from birth to their fifth birthday (or the end of reception year in school).

In the meantime, the government continued identifying the extent and range of adverse effects on children's outcomes across different domains. These included health disadvantage, teenage pregnancy, drug or alcohol abuse, poor nutrition and poverty. Tackling all of society's challenges is a complex process and few of the initiatives had the desired effect in the time-scale expected. However, the exploration and data gathering did highlight some key issues. For example, it was discovered that having a statement of special educational needs did not ensure a smooth path through the education system. Children with statements of special educational needs, then as now, were more likely to receive a fixed term period exclusion; predictably the majority of these related to children recognized as having behavioural, emotional and social difficulties (DfE 2012).

Collaboration between services

The 2003 *Every Child Matters* Green Paper (HMSO 2003: 5), in part a response to the death of Victoria Climbé, repeated calls for the key agencies of education, health, social care, and police services to work more closely together to protect vulnerable children. A series of case reviews identified problems including:

- failure to intervene early enough
- poor communication and coordination between services
- lack of accountability
- poor management
- poor training
- over-stretched staff

However, this was not just a response for those children in highest need but also to improve the quality of life and well-being of all children. Five specific outcomes were established to drive improvement across all services working with children.

1 Being healthy: enjoying good physical and mental health and living a healthy lifestyle
2 Staying safe: being protected from harm and neglect

3 Enjoying and achieving: getting the most out of life and developing the skills for adulthood
4 Making a positive contribution: being involved with the community and society and not engaging in anti-social or offending behaviour
5 Economic well-being: not being prevented by economic disadvantage from achieving their full potential

Local authority services relating to children were now brought together under one Director. A Director of Children's Services would oversee local authority work; a local Safeguarding Board would bring together key personnel in each area to liaise, review and improve local services to protect children. The data that was included in the Green Paper highlighted that there were 50–100 child deaths per year from abuse or neglect and 25,700 children on the child protection register (DfES, 2003: 20).

The Common Assessment Framework (CWDC 2006) was intended to facilitate early identification of a child's needs, while recognizing the holistic view of the child's life and the interrelatedness of their needs with their family circumstances. Ideally, the Common Assessment Framework (CAF) (DfE 2012) form would be completed with the family, providing an opportunity to bring together relevant services in a coordinated way to support and review progress. Importantly, families themselves were also able to request that a CAF be completed to recognize their needs and coordinate appropriate support.

The CAF was intended to ensure information was appropriately communicated across agencies, with a 'lead professional' ensuring interventions complemented each other, in both timing and content. Schools and Children's Centres were identified as sites for multi-agency working, increasing accessibility of professionals and support opportunities. The role of the private and voluntary sector was significantly raised as local groups were included in the range of support available for families, complementing statutory services.

Continued dissatisfaction was also being voiced about the support for children with special educational needs who were educated in mainstream schools. The Audit Commission (2002) issued a report reviewing provision for children with special needs which highlighted that:

- Too many children waited too long to have their needs met.
- Children who should be taught in mainstream schools were turned away and staff felt ill equipped to meet their needs.
- Special schools were uncertain of their future role.
- There was variation in the level of support and quality of provision of different local authorities.

Four areas were highlighted for improvement

- early intervention, including access to suitable childcare
- removing barriers to learning, with inclusive practice included in every school and early years setting
- raising expectations and achievement, developing adult skills and focusing on progress
- delivering improvements in partnership with parents

As an example of effective practice, the Early Support Programme Pilot, originally developed with parents of children with hearing impairment, was extended nationally to support early identification of special educational needs and early intervention from birth. The Early Support Programme is based on 10 principles:

1 The uniqueness of children, young people and their families is valued and provided for.
2 An integrated assessment, planning and review process is provided in partnership with children, young people and families.
3 Service delivery is holistic, co-ordinated, seamless and supported by key working.
4 Continuity of care is maintained through different stages of a child's life and through preparation for adulthood.
5 Children's and young people's learning and development are monitored and promoted.
6 Children, young people and families are able to make informed choices.
7 Wherever possible, children, young people and their families are able to live 'ordinary' lives.
8 Children, young people and families are involved in shaping, developing and evaluating the services they use.
9 Multi-agency working practices and systems are integrated.
10 Children, young people and families can be confident that the people working with them have the appropriate training, skills, knowledge and experience (www.ncb.org/earlysupport).

Some local authorities implemented the Early Support Programme to support families of children with the highest level of needs. Others used the model as a template for all special educational needs support.

Working towards an inclusive society

Amid these many new ways of working, the awareness of equalities continued to be debated and challenged. In 2006 the Equalities Act made it unlawful to discriminate against an individual on the grounds of their age, disability, gender, gender reassignment, race, religion or belief, or sexual orientation. This Act was intended to communicate the aim of developing a society in which:

- people's ability to achieve their potential is not limited by prejudice or discrimination
- there is respect for and protection of each individual's human rights
- there is respect for the dignity and worth of each individual
- each individual has an equal opportunity to participate in society
- there is mutual respect between groups based on understanding and valuing of diversity and on shared respect for equality and human rights

Although this was further strengthened by the 2010 Equalities Act, with publicly funded bodies required to promote equality of opportunity, the day-to-day reality is undoubtedly still a work in progress.

It was not just education which was affected; links were being forged between legislation for all three main agencies with responsibilities for children. In 2008 the Children and Young Persons Act promoted the well-being of children. It revised the functions of social services and established funded 'short breaks' for carers of children with disabilities. As far as health was concerned, the 2009 Healthy Child Programme aimed to support:

- strong parent–child attachment and positive parenting, leading to better social and emotional well-being among children
- the application of new information about neurological development
- an emphasis on integrated services and focus on vulnerable families
- the consideration with families of the risk and protective factors relevant to their child's development
- working towards an integrated 'two-year review' through integrated working with Children's Centres and general practice

The 2011 Health Visitor Implementation Plan articulated the key message as creating,

> A service vision, model and service offer to families for health visiting services that deliver the Healthy Child Programme and are aligned with Sure Start Children's Centres, the Family Nurse Partnership, early years, early intervention services and the new Mental Health Strategy.
>
> (DoH 2011: 20)

These were promising steps towards real integrated working, at least in early years. This cross-agency focus on the complexities of disadvantage, poverty and poor outcomes for children was informed by a series of complementary reports highlighting early intervention as an investment in a secure start in life for children.

In her report, *The Early Years: Foundations for life, health and learning* (DfE 2011a) which reviewed the Early Years Foundation Stage, Dame Clare Tickell cited evidence of 'international recognition and plaudits' for the Early Years Foundation Stage. But although outcomes for young children had improved, there was no time for complacency as 44 per cent were still not reaching a 'good level of development' by the time they were 5 years old. She made 46 recommendations for improvement including:

- an increasing emphasis on working with parents
- a check on progress for 2-year-olds which included development in personal, social and emotional development (PSED), communication and language and physical development
- the 2-year check was to be shared with health visitors and included as an insert in the 'Red Book', which raised its profile
- the identification of the 'Prime' and specific areas of learning in the EYFS
- a reduction in bureaucracy through the slimming down of the early learning goals and profile
- simplifying and improving available practitioner qualifications for early years

Also in 2010 *The Marmot Review: Fair society, healthy lives* (Marmot 2010) explored the factors leading to health inequalities. It identified some interacting complexities such as:

- having enough money to live healthily
- a safe neighbourhood with positive support from family and friends
- a healthy lifestyle including not smoking, eating well and exercising
- biological factors in family history

All of these were recognized to be influenced by social position, education, occupation, income, gender, ethnicity and race.

Social care too was under the spotlight as the Munro Report (DfE, 2011b: 6) reviewed social care practice, child protection, early intervention and information sharing. Munro found worrying trends, citing systems being used to shift blame, rather than support individual accountability for judgements. This was recognized as signs of a service under pressure. Levels of qualification, difficulties in recruitment and overwhelming workloads were acknowledged as reducing the effectiveness of the service. The way forward was seen as refocusing social care practice on valuing professional expertise, and the ability of suitably qualified professionals to make judgements in a child's best interest.

A common purpose?

Continuing the theme of early influences on later lives, the MPs Frank Field and Graham Allen each produced reports exploring the current risks to children's life chances. Field's report, *The Foundation Years* (Cabinet Office 2010) suggested that the first five years of a child's life were a predictor of future development and achievement. This was not just about education but included maternal health, stress-free pregnancy and the importance of secure loving and responsive relationships with clear boundaries. A central part of a child's positive early experiences would include opportunities for cognitive, language and social emotional development.

Field's recommendation was for high quality, community-based support from Children's Centres targeting the most disadvantaged children and their families. The previous significant investment and interventions were noted but quality was still found to be variable and the impact seldom rigorously evaluated. Field's report was followed up by *Early Intervention: The next steps* (Allen 2011) which called for cross-party co-operation and unusually, did not recommended further legislation or an increase in spending.

The notion of meeting the social and emotional needs of young children as a protective factor contributing to future resilience and success in life was a recurrent theme at this time. This was again linked to concerns about poverty. The 2010 Child Poverty Act (HMSO 2010) followed as a response to the increasing awareness of the detrimental impact of poverty on children's life chances. Although the number of children living in relative income poverty was reduced from 3.4 million in 1998/99 to 2.3 million in 2010/11, the target of 1.7 million was not met. The change to the Coalition government in 2010 redirected attention to the causes of poverty, suggesting that the approach of the previous administration had been simplistic (DWP/DfE 2012).

Following this, the Coalition government produced an agenda for a complete overhaul of legislation relating to children and families. This included the special educational needs and disabilities system. The statutory assessment process was perceived as cumbersome, bureaucratic and still leading to too many expensive tribunals. The 2011 SEN Green Paper, *Support and Aspiration* (DfE 2011) set out an array of new proposals including:

- early identification through a single early years setting and school-based category of SEN
- a single assessment process which replaced the 'Statement of Special Educational Needs' with an Education, Health and Care Plan developed with parents and having the same statutory protection as the statement of SEN

- more control for parents including transparency via local authorities setting out their 'local offer' of services available for children with special educational needs, with an option of a personal budget to enable them to select and manage support for their child
- reduced bureaucracy, removing the bias towards inclusion, strengthening parental choice, and enabling the voluntary and community sector to contribute to assessments for the Education, Health and Care Plans
- support for parents from the birth of children with disabilities

A group of local authorities became 'pathfinders' to test out the reforms and the implications for policy and practice. The pathfinder programmes ran for 18 months and their experiences informed the final legislation.

The revised EYFS

Following the Tickell review, a revised EYFS was implemented in 2012. The new document consisted of the statutory framework with further guidance: *Development Matters*, revised by the British Association for Early Childhood Education (2012). The promised progress check for 2-year-olds was included but omitting the direct involvement of Health Visitors. However, pilot programmes trialling the integrated reviews were established around the country with a view to later implementation. As such, the education progress checks take place when a child is between 24 and 36 months and aim to:

- review development in the three Prime Areas (referred to previously)
- enable parents and practitioners to understand the child's needs and plan to meet them at home and in the setting
- raise awareness of both strengths and where progress is less than expected
- describe the actions to be taken to address developmental concerns
  (NCB 2013a: 3)

Local arrangements between EYFS providers and health colleagues increasingly coordinate or integrate this with the Healthy Child Programme that aims to:

- help parents develop a strong bond with children
- encourage care that keeps children healthy and safe
- protect children from serious diseases, through screening and immunization
- reduce childhood obesity by promoting healthy eating and physical activity

- encourage mothers to breastfeed
- identify problems in children's health and development (for example, learning difficulties) and safety (for example, parental neglect) so that they can get help with their problems as early as possible
- make sure children are prepared for school
- identify and help children with problems that might affect their chances later in life (available from www.gov.uk updated Feb. 2014)

A further opportunity to identify concerns in a child's developmental progress will be the new baseline assessment on entry to reception classes beginning in 2015 and it is intended that this will also be linked to 'low prior attainment funding' to facilitate appropriate interventions.

The revised Early Years Foundation Stage Profile (DfE 2013a), in use currently assesses progress at the end of the reception year leading to judgements about children's progress towards 17 Early Learning Goals (ELGs). Previous profile arrangements were thought to be too onerous so the process was simplified. The judgement reflects the child's attainment, in relation to the ELGs as emerging (not achieving), expected (achieving) or exceeding (going beyond expectation). In addition, a description of the child's learning characteristics is included. Anxieties in the sector about a trend away from an observationally-based assessment have been somewhat reduced by the concept of 'responsible pedagogy' described in the EYFS Profile handbook and the proviso that,

> Effective assessment can only take place when children have the opportunity to demonstrate their understanding, learning and development in a range of contexts.
>
> (DfE 2013a: 9)

The Children and Families Act (2014)

Bringing together and raising the quality of services for children has been a core aim of legislation since the Warnock Report. The Children and Families Act (2014) is wide-ranging legislation that includes special educational needs. The implementation of the SEND Code of Practice (DfE 2014a) in local authorities is supported by 'Pathfinder Champions' who contribute effective practice from the pilot programmes.

The major changes outlined in the SEND Code of Practice are:

- It applies to those with special educational needs and disabilities from birth to 25 years.
- To ensure parents, children and young people are central to decision-making.

- Local authorities, schools and maintained nursery schools publish their 'local offer' of support for children and young people with special educational needs and disabilities and their families.
- Early identification and early intervention are supported by a graduated approach based on an 'assess, plan, do, review' cycle leading to an Education, Health and Care Plan.
- Joint commissioning (Health, Education and Care agencies) of support is established comprising the 'local offer' and which is responsive to local priorities, with each service being accountable for delivering appropriate aspects of the Education Health and Care Plan (EHCP).

The link with the UN Convention on the Rights of the Child are maintained through the role of the Children's Commissioner having an overview of how agencies are working together to support children. Periodically, comments from children, young people and parents about the 'local offer' must be published along with the local authority's response. There should also be parental involvement in reviewing provision across all local services.

The SEND Code of Practice requires that responsible bodies must use their 'best endeavours' to secure the special educational provision appropriate to the child's needs.

The definitions of special educational needs remain as having:

- a significantly greater difficulty in learning than the majority of others of the same age or
- a disability which prevents or hinders them from making use of facilities of a kind generally provided for others of the same age in mainstream schools or mainstream post-16 institutions

In addition, 'a child under compulsory school age has special educational needs if they fall within the definitions above or would do so if the special educational provision was not made for them' (DfE 2014a: 4).

Supporting special educational needs in early years

The early years section of the SEND Code of Practice (DfE 2014a) begins by stating that:

All children are entitled to an education that enables them to:

- achieve the best possible educational and other outcomes
- become confident young children with a growing ability to communicate their own views and ready to make the transition to compulsory education

(DfE 2014a: 68)

The role of leadership is highlighted as

> establishing and maintaining a culture of high expectations: a culture that expects those working directly with children . . . with SEN to include them in all the opportunities available to other children: to facilitate their participation; and ensure that they achieve well.
>
> (DfE 2014a: 16)

This reference to high quality provision and effective leadership raises the issue of appropriate support and training – now a requirement for local authorities which are 'to promote inclusion and secure relevant expertise among early years providers' (DfE 2014a: 58). Each EYFS setting is expected to identify a staff member to take responsibility for implementing the setting arrangements for supporting children with SEN. As with other phases of education it would be reasonable to expect the role of special educational needs coordinator (SENCO) to be recognized as a leadership role.

The 'assess, plan, do, review' cycle

The graduated response is now depicted as an increasingly detailed 'assess, plan, do, review' cycle. There is no requirement for Individual Education Plans but similar evidence of interventions, impact on progress and accessing support beyond the setting is required. Local authorities (LAs) continue to fund specialist placement and necessary transport and applications must be made to them for a child or young person's Education, Health and Care Plan (EHCP). The assess, plan, do, review cycle is expected to continue and will include multi-agency representation when an EHCP is in place.

The content of the EHC Plan must specify the following:

- the views, interests and aspirations of the child, parents or young person
- the child's special educational needs
- the health and social care needs and provision
- the intended outcomes of interventions
- the provision required
- the name of school or type of school the child is to attend (once the LA has consulted with the governing body)
- the arrangements regarding personal budgets
- the advice and information gathered during the assessment

(DfE 2014a: 153–8)

As with previous legislation there will be some positive impact, unintended consequences and some opportunities missed to improve the experience of children and their families. In terms of early years, the reiteration of the EYFS principles in the statutory framework secures the hard-won recognition that high quality EYFS practice is recognized as effective inclusive practice.

Key Points

- Joint commissioning among Health, Education and Care agencies raises expectations of achieving integrated working
- Poor outcomes for children are brought about by a complex mix of risk factors
- Tensions between identifying and providing for children with SEN remain, though joint commissioning may lead to increasingly responsive provision

PART 2
The enabling environment: what does success look like?

4 The role of the SENCO

Chapter themes

- The role of the SENCO as a leader
- Improving quality for children with SEND improves quality for all children
- Using one system for observation, assessment and planning for all children including those with SEND is most effective

In the statutory framework for the EYFS the principle positing that:

> Children learn and develop well in enabling environments, in which their experiences respond to their individual needs and there is strong partnership between practitioners and parents and/or carers
>
> (DfE 2014: 6)

represents a particular poignancy in relation to children with special educational needs or disabilities.

It is clearly the responsibility of the leaders and managers in a setting to build a culture of high expectations and continuously improving quality. The SENCO also has a role as a leader of practice and an advocate for inclusion. While all early years providers are expected to identify a SENCO, maintained nursery schools must have a designated teacher, with the prescribed SENCO qualification or relevant experience (DfE 2014: 77).

The SEND Code of Practice (DfE 2014a) describes the role of the SENCO in the early years as:

- ensuring all practitioners in the setting understand their responsibilities to children with SEN and the setting's approach to identifying and meeting SEN
- advising and supporting colleagues
- ensuring parents are closely involved throughout and that their insights inform action taken by the setting
- liaising with professionals or agencies beyond the setting

This identifies the SENCO as a significant influence in establishing and implementing the setting's SEN support. This is not the only person to work with children with special educational needs and disabilities but they are the advocate, mediator and facilitator of the process. In high quality provision this happens through:

- coaching, mentoring and supervising colleagues in providing SEN support
- using existing observation, assessment and planning systems as early warning indicators of emerging needs as well as areas where setting practice needs improvement
- establishing positive relationships with all parents and families
- coordinating provision for children with SEND, including through transitions
- having a working knowledge of and ideally contributing to the relevant Local Offer (including adjoining LAs where appropriate)
- initiating positive contact with a range of local professionals, not just in response to an individual child's needs but as a source of professional development for themselves and colleagues

A recent Parliamentary Inquiry report parent survey found that 41 per cent of parent carers were not accessing their full entitlement of free early education for their child who had special educational needs or disabilities (Contact a Family 2014: 25). The barriers that prevent parents and children accessing early years provision are varied but include:

- lack of EYFS provision in particular areas
- difficulties with physical access
- activities and expectations not tailored to individual need
- staff inadequately trained or lacking confidence
- individual and collective practitioner attitude

Although sufficiency of provision is mainly a local authority responsibility, the SENCO, with leaders and managers, is able to influence the remaining barriers. The concept of making 'anticipatory' reasonable adjustments was established in the Special Educational Needs and Disability Discrimination Act 2001 (HMSO 2001: 13) meaning that the needs of those with special educational needs or disabilities who may attend in the future need to be considered in any plans to develop provision. This would include any physical changes to buildings but also reviews of planning, recording and assessment that could be improved using an SEND perspective.

Beyond the practical provision the most valuable aspect of provision is that the practitioners need to be nurtured and supported to acquire inclusive attitudes. Attitude and appropriate training are closely linked, as demonstrated earlier in discussions of the historical perspective; increasing knowledge has led to greater inclusion. Most discrimination is an expression of fear, anxiety and lack of understanding. Although one advocate for inclusion in a setting can have a significant impact, if it is a central tenet of leadership communicated through all interactions it becomes the embedded culture. All practitioners are responsible for all children so must interact appropriately with all children. The culture of the setting must support adult and child learning in a coherent way based on the inclusive principles of the EYFS.

Tracking progress: when should I be concerned?

The SEND Code of Practice (DfE 2014a: 74) advocates an 'assess, plan, do, review' cycle which fits easily with the familiar EYFS observation, assessment and planning process. The anxiety for practitioners in early years, given that children develop at different rates is at what point they should be concerned and begin to consider the possibility that a child might have special educational needs. Feeling confident about this judgement is reliant on gathering appropriate evidence, knowing the child, including what is happening for them currently, informed by a secure understanding of typical child development.

The SEND Code of Practice (DfE 2014a: 74) lists the following as areas of need:

- Communication and interaction
  - Speech, language, social use of language, relating to others
- Cognition and learning
  - Learning difficulties from moderate to profound and complex
- Social, emotional and mental health
  - Withdrawn, isolated, challenging, anxiety, depression, disorders: Attention Deficit Disorder (ADD) Attention Deficit, Hyperactive, Disorder (ADHD), attachment disorder

- Sensory and/or physical needs

  ○ Visual, hearing, multi-sensory impairment, physical disability

These descriptions support the need to consider the inter-relatedness of the Prime Areas but are also themselves inter-related. Children's needs do not fit into neat categories and interventions must be considered starting from the child's needs, not the broad area of need.

Tracking each child's progress, using *Development Matters* (Early Education 2012) and *Early Years Outcomes* (DfE 2013) will provide a sound basis for monitoring, understanding and responding to individual patterns of development. Each setting will have developed systems which enable them to 'know precisely where children with SEN are in their learning and development' (DfE 2014a: 14). Naturally, effective practice would lead to this being true for all children in EYFS.

Use of a detailed tracking system should be flexible enough to allow for:

- noting individual children's progress in each area of learning
- an overview of each child's relative progress across the Prime Areas of learning
- an overview of each child's relative progress across the prime and specific areas of learning
- regular overview of specific groups of children's progress such as, boys, girls, those with English as an additional language, locally relevant ethnic minorities or summer-born children
- regular overview of comparison of year-on-year cohort progress, for example, did the 2-year-olds in 2013 make similar progress to those in 2014?

Being able to scrutinize progress data in this range of ways enables close monitoring of individual progress, creates a picture of what is usual for this setting and provides evidence of its effectiveness in supporting particular groups of children. Overall this data is also crucial for reviewing the quality and effectiveness of the provision.

Assess, plan, do, review

In the EYFS, where often children's needs are emerging, the initial assessments will mainly consist of:

- practitioner observations
- parent observations

- SENCO observations
- evidence of analysis and joint decision-making with parents

Where there is continuing or increasing concern, advice will be sought beyond the setting, with parental agreement.

For children with special educational needs using more detailed planning evidences our increasing understanding of their approach to learning and the strategies we are using to support them. At this individual level plans need to detail next steps, collate views, including those of the child and their parent, and review progress (for examples, see Appendices 4 and 5) effectively in conjunction with existing planning systems to reduce duplication. Previously these plans were known as Individual Education Plans but in EYFS the term Play Plans, with a format more closely linked to learning journals and 'All about Me' information have developed. Knowing which of the strategies, approaches and interventions are most effective for individual children ensures that time and effort are not wasted. The idea of a 'graduated response' (which begins with low-level intervention and increases in intensity as required to meet the child's needs) in the SEND Code of Practice (DfE 2014a) is clearly linked to the active monitoring of the impact of the strategies employed. The underpinning principle is that the interventions must give the child the 'best possible chance' to make progress. Timescales for review may vary but should reflect realistic expectations and previous patterns of progress demonstrated by the child.

The observation-based planning process in EYFS provides evidence of a child's progress and next steps in each area of learning. Tracking this progress offers an overview of a child's development across the areas of learning. Regular discussions with parents, supervision and staff meetings allow reflection on the expected and the actual progress the child has made. The progress check for 2-year-olds and the Foundation Stage Profile at the end of the reception year are more formal opportunities to review a child's development. Bringing together this information with the child's parents informs discussion about the reasons for the specific rates and patterns of progress. From this evidence base, judgements can be made about whether additional support may be required. If progress is not as expected, clearly it is the provision (not the child) that should be adapted and made flexible to better meet their needs.

The SENCO

As outlined previously, the special educational needs coordinator (SENCO) plays a pivotal role in an early years setting. The responsibilities associated with the role can feel daunting but, as this first case study shows, having effective systems can lead to consistency and collaborative working in the setting. Case study 4:1 illustrates:

- the importance of the SENCO developing positive relationships with all parents
- strong links between the SENCO and Key Person: ensuring children's needs are met
- specific aspects of the SENCO role

Case study 4:1 Early identification and intervention

Interacting with new children and their families

The SENCO (who also fulfils a job-share role) interacts with all new children and their families as a natural part of setting routines. From September to December the focus is on collating observations and getting to know each child, being alert to emerging strengths and difficulties. The SEN support approach includes:

Communication between the practitioner and SENCO

- Regular conversations and concerns recorded in a central notebook
- Practitioners collect observational evidence about learning, development and children's progress
- Once three concerns are raised, joint observations and discussions with the Key Person takes place, suggesting specific strategies or approaches
- The Key Person is supported to reflect on conversations with parents and ways to ensure realistic expectations of the child at home and in the setting
- Key Person discussions with parents take place termly alongside ongoing contact
- Joint meetings with the Key Person, SENCO and parent
- Discussions at staff meetings explore different perspectives giving a holistic view and common understanding of the family context and any key events that may influence the child's progress. This 'shared intelligence' allows all practitioners to respond sensitively to each child's needs in an informed way

Preparing for future multi-agency assessment

- Parental permission to involve the Early Years Team is ideally secured in the Autumn term enabling submission to the February SEN Panel. This allows time for application for specialist placement or support for transition to school

Specific aspects of the SENCO role

- Liaising with external support services and other settings
- Having knowledge of LA procedures and funding implications
- Additional form-filling related to referral to other services
- Reviewing external reports and maintaining links with a range of professionals
- Coaching and mentoring Key Person colleagues
- Moderating decisions in relation to SEN support
- Maintaining consistency of setting SEN support policies in relation to the diverse needs of the children

Putting the SEND Code into practice

The SENCO can be a strong influence in improving practice to the benefit of all children, particularly through devising responsive strategies and collaborating with parents to enhance children's learning. Existing observation, assessment and planning systems in EYFS can be used by the SENCO with colleagues to recognize emerging needs. The systems for observation, assessment and planning for all children need to complement the 'assess, plan, do, review' graduated response of SEN support, thus reducing any unnecessary repetition of record keeping (DfE 2014a: 75).

Further, the SENCO has to maintain links to advice and support beyond the setting ensuring that appropriate help is accessed or signposted in a timely way. This requires a proactive approach involving making contact and engaging education, health and social care professionals not only in relation to a specific child but using ongoing engagement to improve practice in the setting. SENCOs are also role models in supporting colleagues to increase their professional skills in working with children and their families. Taken together, these aspects of the role highlight the advantage of the SENCO being directly involved in the leadership and management of the provision.

Learning Points

- Planning and assessment systems for all children, including those with SEN, should be coherent and not require unnecessary repetition
- An effective SENCO also has a leadership role in improving practice in all aspects of early years provision
- Maintaining relationships and communication with services beyond the setting, not simply in response to an individual child's need, is a useful strategy to develop setting practice and expertise

---

Things to think about

- In what ways does the SENCO in your setting lead effective practice for all children?
- One system of observation, assessment and planning should be effective for all children, including those with identified needs where more detail will be necessary. To what extent is this the case in your setting?
- In what way have you recently used links with other agencies to support professional development for individual practitioners? For example, through linking with health visitors, speech and language, or occupational therapists

---

Striving to meet individual needs

With 78 per cent of families in England using early years child care (Ipsos MORI survey 2011 available on gov.uk) the private, voluntary and independent (PVI) sector plays a very important role in supporting children in EYFS including those with special educational needs. Therefore, it is worth reflecting on how we articulate our practice in relation to special educational needs. Case study 4:2 outlines how a nursery school uses internal processes and links beyond the setting as they strive to meet individual children's needs.

This is a 'pack away' setting in a church hall in a London Borough. There are 15 staff and 60 children on the roll. The owner, Alison, sees recognizing and meeting the needs of each individual child as central to the ethos of her nursery school. A marker of success for the team is that children make a successful transition into their respective schools with appropriate support in place, especially if any special educational need has been identified during their time at the setting. The special educational needs coordinators (SENCOs), Rachel and Chris, take the lead in this process. The SENCO role is currently a job share and the combined experience of the two practitioners underpins the high staff confidence in working with children with special educational needs.

This case study illustrates:

- the SENCO role as part of 'a clear approach to identifying and responding to SEN' (DfE 2014a: 68)
- coordinating internal and external processes
- early identification in the area of 'communication and interaction needs'

- the inherent frustrations and tensions between the early identification of a child's needs and predicting and accessing appropriate support

Case study 4:2 The SENCO role

Identifying and responding to SEN

All staff are responsible for all children and a comprehensive Key Person approach ensures continuity of care and nurture for each child. The SENCOs, Chris and Rachel, are proactive in building positive relationships with all parents. They support colleagues in their interactions with parents especially if a child has special educational needs.

Caroline, a Key Person, raised concerns with the SENCOs about Josh's social communication progress. She observed that while his vocabulary was increasing, his verbal language seemed stilted, repetitive and he sometimes repeated a question he had been asked rather than offering an answer. Socially he tended to engage in solitary activities, with varying tolerance of other children being near him as he played. Although Caroline had talked with his parents about her observations, they did not have concerns, feeling that he was happy and making progress with other areas of learning. Caroline, Chris and Alison, began a gentle, but planned series of conversations with Josh's parents, highlighting observations and revealing monitoring of Josh's progress in all areas of learning. An overview of Josh's progress showed a pattern emerging which supported Caroline's concerns about his development. These conversations also introduced the idea that if additional help or advice were needed in the future, Josh's parents and the SENCO could contact the local authority's Early Years Team.

Developing a common understanding with parents

Chris and Caroline continued planning 'next steps' for Josh, carefully tuning into his individual interests and approaches to learning described through the characteristics of effective learning. His parents were very engaged and, as they shared observations, there developed a balanced understanding of Josh's strengths and the specific help he needed. It was decided that support for shared interaction might be best managed in small group times, when Josh would be given the 'best possible chance' of coping with activities alongside other children. His parents increasingly recognized Josh's particular needs and agreed with Chris that support from the local authority would be helpful.

Local authority support

After a wait of about 4–5 weeks an observation visit from the LA Early Years Team took place. This was a crucial step in confirming the extent of Josh's difficulties. In this authority it was indicated that a child's development must be at least 12 months behind their age in more than one area of development before additional support or application for multi-agency assessment could be considered.

Over a period of 12 months, Caroline and Chris, along with Josh's parents, collected evidence of the impact of their intervention strategies, and monitored Josh's progress. The Early Years Team confirmed the SENCO's concerns and referred the setting to the services of the Educational Psychology Service since Josh was due to go to school in September. However, in June the setting was still awaiting a visit from the educational psychologist to observe Josh. Although his parents and practitioners expected Josh to require further support in school, the LA view was that the school should be able to meet Josh's needs adequately from existing special educational needs funding and that therefore no further action was required.

Putting the SEND Code into practice

Case study 4:2 shows how practitioners strive to make their setting responsive to children and families but also anticipate the level of support that may be needed on transition to school. Tensions can arise among different perceptions of the support needed by the child in one setting compared to another as well as local authority expectations of what schools can provide. The decision to undertake a multi-assessment leading to an Education, Health and Care Plan is based on a situation where, despite 'relevant and purposeful action' being taken 'over a sustained period' to identify and meet a child's needs, they have not made expected progress. The local authority will take into account a range of evidence relevant to a particular child but will also expect that schools and settings will use their 'best endeavours' to meet a child's needs within their own resources, whether financial or physical. In this situation there was recognition of the successful support provided by the nursery and an expectation from the local authority that the school could accommodate the child's needs without recourse to a multi-agency assessment. Previously practitioners were often concerned that schools would refuse entry to a child with SEN if they did not have a Statement of Special Educational Needs already in place. But, the SEND Code of Practice 2014 requires that school admission authorities:

- must consider applications from parents of children who have SEN but do not have an EHC plan on the basis of the school's published admissions criteria
- must not refuse to admit a child who has SEN but does not have an EHC plan because they do not feel able to cater for those needs
- must not refuse to admit a child on the grounds that they do not have an EHC plan

(DfE 2014a: 15)

Learning Points

- Considering the implications of external timescales such as allocation of places at specialist provision is important so that the setting processes can complement these
- Understanding the different perspectives of a school, local authority or EYFS setting can prevent frustrations and tensions
- Keeping parents central to decision-making is a long-term investment enabling parental confidence as they advocate for their child and proactively access services beyond the EYFS setting

---

Things to think about

- What are the timescales and significant decision-making steps towards an Education, Health and Care Plan in your area?
- In what ways do your internal, observation, assessment, planning, early identification and intervention processes link with the route to an Education, Health and Care Plan should this be necessary?
- What forms of evidence from your provision are most useful for other agencies to understand clearly a child's strengths and any concerns about their development?

Communicating our purpose beyond the setting

Both the previous case studies mentioned the importance of the SENCO's relationships with all parents. Those new to the role often feel anxious and dread conversations with parents about a child's emerging needs. They are also often surprised by the range of parents' reactions to their observations.

In Case study 4:3 Lyndsey, a very experienced SENCO, articulates her thoughts about:

- seeing the relationship with parents as a two-way process
- trying to see things from each parent's perspective
- being flexible in problem solving
- thinking beyond EYFS

Case study 4:3 Tuning into parents

Working sensitively with parents

Communication with parents is always two-way; as you listen carefully to their thinking, they are getting to know and trust you. Working sensitively alongside the parents enables recognition that the child's condition is not going to disappear, without either improving or worsening. The world is a difficult place; children will get infections, fall over and sometimes be hurt by other children. All children will have these experiences at some time. For some parents of children with additional needs a focus on the normality of life gives them strength and empowers them. However, other parents will want to wrap up their children in cotton wool and their concerns and desires to protect their children should always be listened to and understood.

Parents bring established views of their children, including tensions between family members about the child's needs. This is true of all children not just those with special educational needs. Parents also often report feelings of guilt, blame and shame, about their child's condition or behaviour. For parents who protectively carry their child into the setting, it is a very big step to think about letting them walk by themselves, because they fear they will be jostled or bumped. Solutions such as arriving five minutes later when there are fewer children around are simple yet effective antidotes to these fears. Allowing their child to walk a few steps through the door enables parents and their child to build their confidence gradually.

Often practitioners are able to take the longer-term view as they have previously experienced parents' fear and emotions, whilst for parents this may feel a major step alongside their uncertainty about how their child's life is likely to develop. Shared discussions can provide insights into parents' current feelings and sensitively engaging with parents is necessary if trust is to be secured between parents and professionals.

Transition is a particularly anxious time for all children, parents and practitioners. Our ability to articulate our common purpose across the transition can be a powerful support for a child but also their parents, particularly when a child has special educational needs or disabilities. Practitioners who have worked with a child and their family over time develop strategies and approaches increasingly tailored to meet their specific needs. The practitioner's detailed learning about the child is immensely valuable in facilitating a successful transition to their next setting. The challenge is communicating the necessary information appropriately and in an accessible way. As a rule of thumb, the higher a child's level of need, the greater the importance of a face-to-face discussion.

In reality, there are times when, with the best of intentions things are still difficult for the child and their family. Case study 4:4 illustrates:

- the importance of recognizing a common purpose as a means of enabling creative problem-solving for a child whose needs are in the area of 'social, emotional and mental health'
- keeping the focus on the child and their family as decision-makers in the process
- face-to-face communication involving all key decision-makers can bring about solutions unlikely to arise from letter, email or phone contact

---

Case study 4:4 Doing the best we can for each child

Transition from nursery to primary school

Aleisha arrived at a private day nursery in April, having been excluded from a Nursery School following concerns about her behaviour. She moved to the local school reception class in September after four months attendance at the day nursery.

In October, Aleisha's very distressed mother contacted the nursery about the exclusion. She was due to return to school after half-term to attend for 2½ hours each morning pending a referral to a support service.

A visit to the school was arranged by the day nursery SENCO and the nursery owner/manager to understand the problems the school faced. This ensured the nursery understood the strategies used in school in order to inform future practice.

The meeting with Aleisha's teacher was reported as extremely tense and it was apparent that the expectation was that the nursery staff would pass judgement on the school's approach to Aleisha's needs. However, once the nursery's position was made clear and staff demonstrated they were empathetic to the school's challenges, the meeting took on a whole new demeanour. Those present expressed their common goal as 'To do their very best for Aleisha.'

Discussions then focused on Aleisha and her family's needs and on identifying actions in their best interests. There soon developed an openness and positivity, previously lacking and staff talked enthusiastically about ways forward. Aleisha's mother was central to these discussions and regarded as the ultimate decision-maker. Together the practitioners worked to provide her with creative possibilities to meet Aleisha's current care and educational needs.

It was agreed that the nursery could facilitate a 1:1 ratio for an interim period of six weeks and Aleisha could attend the nursery full-time. She could then be supported at the Behaviour Support unit, where staff would facilitate school visits, and ease the transition back to her school (mainstream), if and when this was deemed appropriate. The school proposed that they would cover the cost of the full-time nursery place so that Aleisha's parents did not incur any financial burden.

Putting the SEND Code into practice

Together these two case studies illustrate the impact a skilled SENCO can have in understanding and facilitating support, in conjunction with colleagues, yet with parents at the centre of decision-making (DfE 2014a: 76).

Professional respect, especially at times when it feels as though things have gone wrong, can be difficult to establish. In Case study 4:4 the day nursery practitioners took the lead in communicating their empathy and intention to contribute in a positive way. As described, this significantly changed the tone of the discussion. By being solution-focused, the practitioners were able to offer realistic options for Aleisha's mother to consider. With a common purpose both the day nursery and the school were able to contribute to the successful solution, including engaging with advice and support beyond their own organizations.

Learning Points

- Recognizing others' perspectives helps to break down barriers and enables more effective problem-solving

- Thinking together how to 'do the best' for a specific child offers realistic options and creative possibilities
- Keeping parents central to decision-making helps solutions remain practical, supportive and likely to succeed

Things to think about

- What is the most creative solution you have devised recently to support a child in their transition to another setting?
- What would your response have been when Aleisha's mother arrived at nursery after her child had started school if Aleisha had previously attended your setting?
- When preparing for transition, what leads you to decide to organize a face-to-face meeting with parents and practitioners from the 'new' setting?

Improving and developing practice

- How can the SENCO in your setting be more involved in supervision and leadership?
- How confident are your practitioners when articulating the setting's procedures for tracking progress, analysing data and identifying areas of provision needing improvement?
- In what ways have SEN processes improved practice for all children in your setting?

Key Points

- The SENCO role is a strong influence on general setting practice, specifically:
  - collaborating with parents
  - identifying appropriate next steps
  - devising responsive strategies and evidencing impact
  - seeking advice beyond the setting

- coaching and mentoring colleagues
- role modelling effective practice

- Children with SEN often challenge us to improve our practice, as practitioners gain confidence, the SENCO can ensure that this enhances every child's experience
- The SENCO should be involved in planning support for transitions, increasing links with local SEN and mainstream provision

5 EYFS: a principled approach

Chapter themes

- Seeing the world from the child's perspective

- Using knowledgeable observation and sharing thinking with parents and carers to enable problem-solving

- The need for practitioners to challenge existing barriers to inclusion through advocacy and mediation with colleagues, parents and children

The Unique Child in the context of the EYFS

As we saw in Part 1, the journey towards inclusion in early years provision and indeed in society itself has been a long and sometimes difficult one. However, the EYFS statutory framework seeks to provide, 'equality of opportunity and anti-discriminatory practice, ensuring that every child is included and supported.' (DfE 2014: 5). This marks considerable progress from the segregation of the past. As described in Chapter 4 the SENCO in EYFS will have an overview of children's development, monitoring rates and patterns of progress.

Building on the principles of the EYFS, systems and routines in settings commonly include a 'settling-in process'. This process, though necessitating some consistency, must be also responsive to individual children's needs in order to be successful. Practitioners can feel that getting to know a child with special educational needs is somehow different from getting to know a child without additional needs. For example, a child in a wheelchair may be thought of in terms of the challenges in moving the wheelchair around the setting rather than being seen as, Aleisha, a girl, who loves to be outdoors playing in the water. Every child is a unique individual with likes, dislikes, strengths, and challenges. They need adults who enable and engage in communication and who demonstrate sensitive understanding of their intentions, desires and beliefs. Policy in the UK recognizes parents as their child's first educator who should be viewed as knowledgeable advocates for, and skilled communicators with, their children. Therefore, listening carefully to parental views and understanding their communication beyond the spoken words is a core part of professional engagement with parents. EYFS settings use a range of approaches to help get relationships off to a positive start. The following five case studies illustrate how each unique child has been included in the setting they attend and, with their families, genuinely welcomed.

Periods of transition can be challenging and difficult at the best of times since moving from a familiar to an unfamiliar context has an emotional impact on us all. Research cites family, friendships and effective setting practice as significant protective factors for children during transition (Evans et al. 2010: 15). The professionals in Case study 5:1 have used their skill to deeply understand the children and their families so that the process can be responsive to their needs.

The importance of first impressions

The first case study, focusing on 3-year-old Frank, illustrates how valuable home visits can be as preparation for a child's first days in their new setting. It describes how seeing Frank in his own home allowed practitioners to observe him feeling relaxed and in familiar surroundings. The visit established a shared approach between parents and practitioners.

This case study illustrates the importance of:

- listening carefully to parents' views, worries and previous successes
- helping to personalize support for a child who has needs in areas of 'communication and interaction' and 'social, emotional and mental health'
- being flexible in staffing, timings and use of space so that strategies are responsive and sensitive
- making positive links with other groups and provision to support the child and his parents effectively

Case study 5:1 Frank's transition to nursery school

First experiences of nursery school

Concerns had been raised during the home visit about Frank's anxiety with unfamiliar people and places. Through listening to parents' previous experiences practitioners devised an individualized plan for Frank's transition to their setting.

Small steps – coming to the building and playing in the corridor

The first step was to use Frank's favourite play dough activity for daily, short play sessions in the corridor before any attempt was made to encourage him to enter the room to be with other children. This gradually reduced his anxiety about being in a new place. It allowed him to get the feel of the new environment and know the people in it. To ensure continuity for Frank, his Key Person led the corridor play sessions, supported by the SENCO.

The gradual move from the 'safety' of the corridor to the room was carefully managed by moving the play session nearer to the room each time. Parents contributed their observations of Frank's decreasing anxiety levels so that practitioners could also recognize his changing emotions. This temporary and flexible plan of attendance allowed progress without undue distress for Frank or his parents.

Responding to parents' and children's current concerns

Also during the home visit Frank's parents articulated worries about difficulties during mealtimes. In response, the SENCO, with his parents' consent, organized attendance patterns to include Frank in the after-school meal club. This practical support contributed to building social links for Frank.

Putting the SEND Code into practice

Enabling parents to offer insights about their child's development can be challenging (Crowley and Wheeler, in Pugh and Duffy 2014: 223). However, parents are also intrigued to hear about practitioners' observations, especially when their own views have been listened to carefully. By presenting themselves as professionals who were keen to listen, the practitioners helped parents to voice their specialist knowledge and concerns. Using the parents' previous 'successes' to inform the 'settling-in' process for Frank, demonstrated that they were valuing his parents' contribution.

Trust is a key component of a good partnership. In this example, parents trusted the practitioners to have a common purpose of helping Frank make a successful transition. The practitioners earned further trust by using parents' insights to judge the pace of the programme and understand Frank's emotional response. The practitioners demonstrated their ability to think holistically about Frank and his current needs, by extending the flexibility of his attendance to include the after-school meal club. By keeping Frank at the centre of their thinking the adults, parents and practitioners really established a partnership relationship that encouraged sharing of concerns and joint problem-solving.

Learning Points

- For home visits to be successful, they need to be carefully thought through, including how they will be offered; the stated purpose; and how conversations will be responded to and encouraged
- Listening to and valuing parents' specialist knowledge about their child is an investment in the partnership that usually results in long-term gains
- Being familiar with locally based support enables timely and appropriate support to be offered to children and their families

---

Things to think about

- To what extent does your current practice demonstrate sensitive and responsive approaches to the transition from home to setting?
- With which local sources of family support have you successfully engaged parents in the past six months?
- In what ways have you demonstrated how much you value parents' insights and specialist knowledge of their child in the past week?

The Key Person role

Case study 5:2 explores the transition from home to setting where a child's special educational needs have already been identified. Jasmin had received support from the Portage Team to help with her physical, social and communication needs. Support from the Early Years team was not put in place until after Jasmin had begun regularly attending the day nursery. Referrals had been made to occupational health, physiotherapy and speech and language therapy for further support. Knowing that a child who is about to start at nursery or school has significant special educational needs can be a daunting prospect for practitioners as well as for parents and their child. In this case the Key Person reflected on her own knowledge and practice, seeking to ensure that Jasmin would have a really positive start.

This case study illustrates the importance of:

- being proactive as a Key Person in developing your own knowledge and understanding
- observations providing insights about how best to support new learning
- using small 'next steps', gradually building on current success in order to facilitate progress for a child whose needs are in the areas of 'sensory and/or physical' and 'social, emotional and mental health'

Case study 5:2 Jasmin begins day nursery

The Key Person role during transition

Maria, the Key Person for Jasmin, remembered vividly how scary it felt having a child with SEN join her group – an anxiety which stemmed from wanting to do her best for Jasmin. The first step was to learn more about Jasmin's identified needs. Before meeting Jasmin or her parents Maria read previous records from Portage, used online research sources and had discussions with the setting's SENCO to add to her existing knowledge.

Working together to make 'inclusion' a reality for everyone

Once Jasmin started attending nursery, the focus, as with all children, was to get to know her as an individual personality. Maria used her observations and interactions during play activities to find out about Jasmin's likes, dislikes and emotional responses to situations. Maria noticed that Jasmin's language development was delayed, that she preferred to play alone and showed a reluctance to join in with other children. Conversations with Jasmin's parents helped establish how to recognize facial expressions and body language indicating when Jasmin was at ease or feeling anxious.

The SENCO/Manager and Maria began detailed planning using play plans which, with the input of the parents, identify the next steps, strategies and activities that would best support Jasmin. From their common knowledge of Jasmin they assessed her skills and social understanding. Together they agreed 'next steps' and how Maria would use familiar situations to give Jasmin the 'best possible chance' to achieve small, achievable targets in her development and learning. The play plan form was used to evidence thinking and decisions made by Jasmin's parents and the nursery team.

Maria used Jasmin's favourite game as a device to gradually involve other children in a collaborative activity. As Jasmin gained confidence in playing alongside others, she also became familiar with their names. The other children benefited from the small group activity and spending time with Jasmin whilst an adult mediated interaction and helped to establish relationships and successful play.

Building coherent links between home and setting

Although Maria took the lead in planning for Jasmin, all adults were responsible for observing and interacting throughout the day. They noticed, over time, that Jasmin made significant progress, becoming more independent and enjoying positive relationships with other children. Through sensitive discussion with Jasmin's parents, similar activities were developed at home to support her progress. This widened to other areas to enhance her physical development based on suggestions from the physiotherapist, and included preparing the table for meals, pouring drinks and offering plates of fruit to others.

Putting the SEND Code into practice

Getting to know a new child in your setting is a skilled job, and understanding their individual pattern of communication and interaction is complex. Knowing that a child who will be attending your setting has an identified special educational need is an opportunity to reflect on and improve your current practice. Whilst reading and researching a specific condition or diagnosis can be helpful, it will only provide general background. No two children will be affected in the same way so parental knowledge is the most valuable source of information. Encouraging parents to feel confident about their articulation of their child's needs is an important part of early conversations with them:

> There is a need to ensure that parents' first experiences of the SEN process are positive. Parents should be encouraged to

engage in a collaborative and consultative approach to their child's development . . .

(White et al. 2010: 23)

Using early conversations to demonstrate that we are keen to learn from parents about their child is a positive step. Giving positive feedback to parents about their own support for their child will also increase their confidence to share future successes as well as concerns.

Learning Points

- Common understanding between home and the setting was consolidated through specific activities and Jasmin's subsequent progress was celebrated as the outcome of a joint effort
- External advice was integrated into nursery practice so that Jasmin was more often included in activities with other children
- Small group activities were seen as supportive for all children; Maria mediated the experiences in order to increase each child's involvement

---

Things to think about

- Which activities do children currently enjoy that could be described to parents? How could this information lead to greater common understanding of each child's progress?
- In what ways have you informed parents about the skills and abilities that particular activities support?
- How/when have you given parents genuine, positive feedback about the support they give to their children?

Meeting the individual needs of the child

Once children are attending an EYFS setting, recognizing their progress helps to ensure appropriate challenges and 'next steps' are offered to support their development. It is clear that not all children will make progress in the same way or at the same time. Practitioners need to know about an individual child's current competencies. For children with additional needs this also ensures that professionals can review evidence and plan appropriately. This, as has been indicated in earlier chapters, is described in the SEND Code of Practice (DfE 2014a) as a graduated response comprising a cycle of:

- Assess
- Plan
- Do
- Review

Through gathering observations and evidence of progress, practitioners, in discussion with parents, will analyse a child's support needs. This evidence provides the basis for 'next steps' which should lead to realistic progress over a specific period of time. The child's views should inform the details of the support on offer. Although the Key Person remains responsible for the day-to-day support of the child, the SENCO is also expected to support and advise as necessary. If the expected progress is not made, observations should reveal what has been learned about the child and their approach to learning. These will inform the next cycle of 'assess, plan, do and review' providing increasing detail and identifying more effective support. If progress is not made over a sustained period of time, external advice from specialists should be sought, with parental agreement.

Case study 5:3 illustrates one setting's approach to tracking children's progress. One planning system is used for all children, enabling continuity and coherence, with increasing detail as necessary to address concerns that arise about an individual child's current progress.

This case study illustrates the importance of:

- establishing and maintaining positive relationships with parents
- involving parents in a collaborative process of identifying and planning for a child's individual needs
- continuity in communication with parents – from day-to-day conversations, through devising and developing play plans, sharing observations and termly learning story reviews
- the use of the 'assess, plan, do, review' cycle

(DfE 2014a: 74)

Case study 5:3 Child awareness process

Reviewing progress

When parents or practitioners express concerns about a child's progress or development, their 'child awareness' process is used. This alerts all practitioners and triggers a process involving 'focused' observations. The staff team meets at the end of each day to talk about their observations. Practitioners' perceptions are gathered and any evidence is explored. As concerns are clarified, possible interventions and forms of support are devised. Play plans with 'next steps' are used: (a) to record support; (b) to identify expected outcomes; and (c) to establish realistic timescales reflecting parents' suggestions and ideas. Together parents and practitioners include the child's expressed views of activities, forms of support, relationships with adults and other children to construct the interventions.

Linking different forms of evidence and record keeping

Within two weeks of any child starting at the nursery a baseline assessment is completed detailing what the child 'can do', that is, reflecting their current competencies. *Development Matters* is used to support assessment in the three Prime Areas of the EYFS. Practitioners then moderate assessments, offer opinions and ideas about children's learning styles and help solve problems for practice through daily discussions.

On a termly basis, video observations are completed for each child and reviewed with parents. These offer a really positive opportunity to acknowledge developmental progress as it is revealed in the process. The ensuing conversations can be emotional, with parents often surprised by the progress their child has made. Parents also gain insight into how activities they have undertaken at home contribute to their child's development and learning. Practitioners also talk about the impact of early intervention strategies.

The tone and manner of these conversations mean they are highly valued by parents and practitioners. The video observation discussions do not stand alone but are part of wider interactions between parents and staff. These discussions are an integral part of the learning stories that celebrate a child's learning, interests and progress. They are in the form of a story book, showing a piece of learning indicative of the child's current competencies. This book goes home and the child and their parents are encouraged to add their comments. Daily conversations lead to further comments being added, reflecting a collective understanding of the child's learning.

Putting the SEND Code into practice

All children come to settings at different points in their development and each child's developmental story is unique. Communication with parents should increase their confidence and understanding of their child's particular developmental story. It is the tone and content of these conversations that establish a positive collaboration. Using the evidence of observations from both home and setting shows respect for parents' perspectives and enables collaborative thinking to develop in order to support their child. This continuity can sustain confidence through some of the more challenging conversations as adults strive to understand a child's specific needs and how these can best be met. As highlighted by Harris and Goodall, engaging parents in their children's learning and development needs must be prioritized, made a two-way process and embedded in the planning of children's learning in order to have most impact (Harris and Goodall 2007: 2). Although systems, even those which are thoughtfully devised can help a setting to run smoothly, the balance between maintaining appropriate records and investing in the quality of relationships can be problematic. It is debatable whether any of the systems in the previous case studies would have been as effective if the practitioners had not been striving to engage positively with parents and children alike.

Learning Points

- Different levels of record-keeping need to be coherent and effectively communicate the story of a child's development
- Record-keeping should also indicate how parents have contributed information – whether or not these are surprises, delights or concerns
- Building parents' confidence in imparting their specialist knowledge, establishes a flow of information between adults who are genuinely interested in a child's progress

Things to think about

- What evidence of how parents have contributed to their child's record or learning journey is currently included in the record-keeping of your setting?
- What are the views of parents about the format of record-keeping you use and the degree of accessibility to this information?
- How do you reflect children's views about how their progress is recorded and what is their contribution to the process?

Pathways to support

Making a first visit to a setting can be a daunting prospect for any parent. Practitioners may only get one chance to engage a particular parent on a supportive journey. In this context every interaction needs to count. Case study 5:4 shows how effective early interactions with parents can lead to appropriate support for children and make a long-term impact on the parents themselves. Children's Centres usually offer a range of different activities for families. It is often the one-off 'drop-in' session that first attracts parents, but it is the welcome they receive that secures further involvement. Indira, recently resident in the UK, reported feeling guilty and isolated from family and friends. She had previously been told, following a traumatic premature birth, that her son Roman 'would probably have some brain injury'. She felt unable to give Roman and his three sisters all the help she thought they needed. She recognized Roman's additional needs but worried the future for him would not be good. She was invited by a Family Support Worker to visit her local Children's Centre.

This case study illustrates the importance of:

- practitioners being knowledgeable about and providing reliable information on local provision
- sensitivity in initial meetings with parents enabling the communication of salient information leading to more targeted support
- parents' confidence being supported by sensitive interactions with staff who help them to recognize their own skills and knowledge
- emerging needs in areas of 'sensory and/or physical needs' 'communication and interaction' and 'cognition and learning'

Case study 5:4 Helping Roman and his family

Pathways to support from 'Stay and Play'

Indira and Roman (aged 23 months) attended the Stay and Play session at the Children's Centre. It was a very busy group with approximately 30 children and their parents present. A practitioner, Leanne, welcomed Indira, showed her around and introduced her to other parents. After only 10–15 minutes Indira was ready to leave, saying the session was too busy. Leanne talked with her about other sessions and activities running at the Children's Centre. Indira said Roman needed quieter sessions because of his special needs. She became very tearful, saying she 'didn't know what to do'.

Possibility thinking

Leanne suggested Indira attend the much quieter Communication through Play (CTP) session. Skilled practitioners ran these sessions, interacting with parents and their children. They would help identify key developments in children's use and understanding of language and help them take part in the activities.

Successful outcomes

Roman and Indira then began attending the CTP sessions regularly. Roman soon began to crawl and gesture to others to communicate his needs. In discussion with Indira and her partner, a referral was made to the Speech and Language and Occupational Therapy Services. Following the outcomes of these referrals and subsequent interventions Roman made significant progress in all three Prime Areas of the EYFS. Indira became confident enough to become a 'parent buddy' for new parents at the group, and then began attending other activities and expressed interest in becoming a 'literacy champion'.

Putting the SEND Code into practice

By being alert to Indira's changing emotion during her first visit Leanne was able to create an opportunity for her to talk more about Roman, his needs and her worries. In addition, Leanne understood enough about the other groups and activities being offered to select one likely to accommodate both Roman's and Indira's needs at this time. This included the implicit understanding that Indira would be welcomed and supported at the group. Importantly, she knew Indira would be able to attend immediately, thus responding to her current worries about Roman's progress.

As a result of the Children and Families Act (2014) local authorities, schools and maintained nurseries are required to publish their 'local offer' of provision for children with special educational needs and their families. This information is set to become an important source of information for practitioners as well as parents. Details of the 'local offer' are included in the SEND Code of Practice (DfE 2014a: 47) and EYFS settings are encouraged to contribute information.

Learning Points

- Making a first visit to a setting can be an emotional experience for parents
- Knowing about current, local and appropriate sources of information helps to improve the quality of the advice and support given to parents of children with special educational needs
- EYFS providers can contact their local authority to contribute to the local offer

Things to think about

- What does the 'local offer' in your area include as a source of independent advice for parents of children with special educational needs?
- In what ways do your nearest maintained nursery and primary school(s) support children with identified special educational needs if they do not have an Education, Health and Care Plan?
- How have you canvassed parents' views of their needs? Which of the parents you are currently working with might be interested in discussion groups run locally related to managing a child's sleep, mealtimes or behaviour?

Collaborative working

The powerfully positive experience of being welcomed and valued in a child's first EYFS setting is one which parents are likely to remember for a lifetime. Equally, a rejection for parents at this early stage can make future engagement with other professionals more difficult. As previously discussed, the quality of interactions is crucial in ensuring timely, sensitive support for children with special educational needs and their families, but the physical environment should also be considered. Case study 5:5 shows how both the emotional and physical environments are intertwined. It emphasizes just how important it is to give time for children to mentally, physically and emotionally 'map' new environments. This case study portrays Mia who is making the transition from day nursery to a nursery school on the same site. Notice how her visual impairment which could be seen as an added challenge in this process is understood and how her needs are accommodated.

The Early Support Materials referred to in this case study which provide a comprehensive range of information and resources are available from the Council for Disabled Children website (www.councilfordisabledchildren.org.uk/earlysupport). The Early Support Development Journals offer a format for building a family record of a child's progress and the support accessed. This is similar but much more comprehensive than the Personal Child Health Record given to all children at birth in the UK (access at www.rcpch.ac.uk). Parents can use these documents to ensure professionals have accurate information and a chronology of events without the need to retell their family story.

This case study illustrates:

- using parents' knowledge of previous events to inform effective strategies and approaches to new situations
- using the Early Support Development Journal to share information between professionals, thus avoiding parents having to retell their stories
- being flexible and responsive in the short term in order to achieve longer-term goals for a child who has needs in the area of 'sensory and/or physical needs'
- engaging with specialists beyond the setting to target support most effectively

Case study 5:5 Mia goes to nursery school

Flexible and responsive support during transition

Mia has bilateral coloboma, resulting in significant visual impairment. She attended the day nursery from 2 years old and during this time her parents were introduced to the Early Support Developmental Journal for children with visual impairment. This was used to record Mia's developmental milestones. Mia's Key Person kept her own log using the same journal, meeting with her parents regularly to talk about progress. In preparation for her transition to the nursery school, the 'old' and 'new' Key Persons used the journal to establish a common understanding of Mia's achievements and progress.

Using shared knowledge and understanding

Adjusting to the much larger spaces indoors and out at nursery school was always likely to be challenging for Mia. To support the physical aspect of transition Mia was given access to the environment when no other children were present and helped to 'map' the new environment. She explored the perimeter of each space talking with her Key Person about each feature she encountered. Gradually, Mia was able to access each area at the same time as other children. The nursery school environment became a familiar, comfortable place for her. The next step was for Mia to negotiate the breakfast and after-school club in the same building so that her parents could continue with their work commitments. Extending her day at nursery school in this way gave Mia complete confidence to use the entire nursery building.

Thinking beyond the setting

The Local Authority Visual Impairment Team provided specific help to support Mia's motor, mobility and literacy skills. Mia was able to access the EYFS and regular formative and summative assessments continued to show how well she was progressing. A key feature of the successful support for Mia was the dedication of her parents and their understanding of the importance of her learning beyond the immediate environment of the school.

Putting the SEND Code into practice

Early diagnosis of a specific condition requires close working between parents and professionals to ensure appropriate support is available in a timely way as a child grows, matures and their needs evolve. Sharing information between settings can cause some anxiety, particularly for parents. Making the purpose clear, celebrating successes as well as recording concerns all help to keep parents central to the process.

By working with Mia's parents, practitioners were able to devise a personalized programme to support her transition. As this is recorded in her Development Journal similar strategies can be considered and adapted for her next transition into school.

Having evidence of these successful strategies:

- avoids using a trial and error approach
- demonstrates trust between parents and practitioners
- builds on previous success
- is familiar and responsive to the child's needs
- reduces anxiety especially for parents and the child involved

---

Learning Points

- Seeing the situation from Mia's perspective directly informed how the transition process could be made responsive to her needs
- The Early Support Development Journal provided joint knowledge of Mia's needs and effective strategies
- Engaging positively with support from external services such as those provided by the LA increased the effectiveness and accuracy of the strategies employed

---

Things to think about

- Early Support Principles and materials complement those of the EYFS; to what extent do they reflect your own practice in supporting children with special educational needs?
- Moving from the familiar to the unfamiliar is an emotional experience whether you are an adult or a child. How flexible have you been in giving children time and opportunity to 'map' the new environment and get the 'feel of the place' when they start at your setting?

Conclusion

The EYFS statutory document (DfE 2014) gives clear messages about the importance of adults at home and in the setting working together to fully understand and meet each child's needs. Further suggestions and guidance in the EYFS (DfES, 2008) materials such as the Principles into Practice cards and in the *Birth to Three Matters Framework* (DfES 2003a) remain relevant and useful to prompt detailed reflection on inclusive early years practice.

As was seen in Part 1, several political agendas have led to the current nature and availability of childcare. However, the purpose for which the EYFS exists is to support the nurture, learning and development of our youngest children. It seems obvious then that we should consider the daily experience of the setting from the child's perspective if we are to develop our practice to be fully inclusive of all children.

A particular characteristic of children with special educational needs or disabilities is that their lives tend to be dominated by relationships with adults. This is not through choice or selection but is explained by the fact that in their desire to be helpful, adults can become a barrier to children building mutually enjoyable peer relationships. Offering 'one-to-one' support can be our first port of call when a child with additional needs joins our setting community. Whilst it may be true that an extra pair of hands will be useful in those early days, the hazards of even implicitly allocating responsibility for one child to one adult need to be considered carefully. The Key Person approach advocated in EYFS recommends there should be closer bonds between the child and one or two named adults; this should clearly be in the context of all adults continuing to have responsibility for all children, whilst maintaining a stronger bond with their 'key children'. Continuity of care is crucial to enabling children to feel emotionally safe. Encouraging positive relationships to develop between children as well as with adults is also part of the social and emotional environment that is created.

Responsive, insightful adults create flexible approaches devised with the child's best interests at heart. This is not to say that this will always be a smooth and simple process. There can be anxieties that existing routines will disintegrate into chaos as staff attempt to implement a separate routine for each child. The reality is that if observation, joint discussion with parents and growing knowledge of the child's approaches to learning are at the heart of decision-making, then routines are more likely to improve rather than deteriorate.

Improving and developing practice

- Having read the last three case studies and reflected on them would it be easier to include Jasmin, Roman or Mia in your setting? Why?
- In what ways could your setting's admission and 'settling-in' process be more responsive to individual children's needs?
- Planning for and recording children's progress are an integral part of EYFS practice. How do play plans for children with SEN fit into your existing systems?

Key Points

- The EYFS is an inclusive framework and supports practitioners to be responsive to all children's needs. A core element is to maintain positive relationships with all adults who are special to the child. Every interaction, no matter how short, makes a difference
- All children have likes, dislikes, strengths and unique personalities, whether they have additional needs or not. Working collaboratively with colleagues and parents helps to moderate judgements

and ensure that each child is given the 'best possible chance' of making progress

- Recording systems such as play plans should be robust enough to highlight both the child's progress and adults' learning about the child's needs and abilities
- Practitioners experience predictable transitions as groups of children move on each term, or each year, but it is salutary to remember that for each child and their parents each new transition is a 'first'. The Key Person and coherent record-keeping should serve as a bridge throughout the transition process whether from home to setting, room to room, setting to setting or setting to school

6 The Prime Areas of Learning in the EYFS and early identification of SEN

Chapter themes

- Alignment of the 'Assess, plan, do review' graduated response with a setting's systems for tracking all children's progress

- Supporting inclusion through the supervision process

- Seeking external advice and support informed by the published 'local offer'

- Gathering evidence, positive information sharing and running multi-agency meetings

Development in children's earliest years is both rapid and intense. Much of this development is common to all children regardless of their geographical or cultural context, in this sense it is 'universal'. In addition, many of the skills and abilities are described as time-sensitive in that they are more easily acquired as part of this early developmental stage rather than later (Evangelou 2009: 14). These universal and time-sensitive areas of development are described as 'Prime Areas of Learning' in EYFS and comprise personal, social and emotional development, communication and language and physical development (DfE 2011: 92).

A crucial issue for early identification of special educational needs is that these three areas of development are interrelated. Our thinking needs to recognize that, for example, being able to move independently will increase opportunities to make social connections rather than being dependent on those who come to you. Displaying emotions, perhaps through crying or smiling communicates with others. Thus relationships evolve, along with gradual understanding of ourselves and others. The development of language, both understood and spoken, enables thinking, communication and coordinating of actions. While *Development Matters* (Early Education 2012) and *Early Years Outcomes* (DfE 2013) provide a guide to typical development in each area of learning, each individual child is different, so our analysis of progress must reflect our holistic understanding of each child.

Knowing the child: Key Person and SENCO collaboration

In being alert to the detail of each child's early development in the Prime Areas, the Key Person has a major role to play. For children with special educational needs the Key Person and SENCO must work collaboratively developing a common understanding of each child.

Extending the collaboration to include parents

Practitioners will usually report that they have very positive relationships with parents. On the other hand, asked which area of their practice causes most concern, they will often reply that it is 'relationships with parents'. This, in my view, indicates just how important these relationships are, but also how difficult it can be to feel confident that we are maintaining high levels of collaboration. It is unrealistic to expect the same level of engagement from all parents, all of the time. As professionals we must take the lead in relationships with parents. We continuously seek to enhance these relationships to ensure the best support for the children in our care. Supervision discussions as described in the EYFS (DfE 2014: 20) provide the ideal forum for reflecting on and exploring concerns about relationships with parents. As such, no practitioner should feel that they are alone making difficult decisions or dealing with emotionally charged situations. As Cook (2013: 36) explains, supervision provides 'the opportunity to stand back ... bringing greater objectivity and insights'. The process of supervision is particularly important for practitioners working with children with special educational needs and their families and 'should foster a culture of mutual support, teamwork and continuous improvement, which encourages the confidential discussion of sensitive issues' (DfE 2014: 20).

As the SENCO and the Key Person review progress, further insights about how the child learns and effective interventions can be gained.

The following case studies illustrate how these elements of practice come together to support Darren and his family. The four case studies illustrate how review meetings are used to summarize progress and plan ways forward together with parents. The first case study shows how these particular aspects of practice work together:

- the Key Person's collaborative working with SENCO

- positive relationships with parents
- tracking individual progress
- supervision

Background to Darren's story

The key adults in Darren's life are:

Mum: Jackie   Dad: Tariq
Key Person: Mandy   SENCO: Jamila

Darren began attending the day nursery when he was 9 months old. He settled well and developed a positive relationship with his Key Person, Mandy. His parents, Jackie and Tariq were very supportive, regularly conversing with the room team. During the 'settling-in period' no particular concerns were raised about his development. As is their usual practice, following the first month of Darren's attendance a review discussion with parents was organized. Mandy and the SENCO, Jamila, were both to attend as they do whenever possible for all children.

Case study 6:1 Preparation for a review meeting

Context: Mandy and Jamila's supervision discussion

During her supervision discussions with Jamila, Mandy identified the significant points she wanted to communicate to Darren's parents. She intended to focus on his progress in the Prime Areas of Learning but also wished to highlight how activities Darren enjoyed were enabling his progress in the specific areas of learning too (i.e. literacy, mathematics, understanding of the world and expressive arts and design). Mandy had completed the overview sheet (see Appendix 3) showing her assessment of Darren's progress in relation to typical development (DfE 2013; Early Education 2012). Jamila and Mandy shared their different experiences of working with Darren, reviewing observations, photographs and his learning journal. Mandy reflected on conversations with Jackie and Tariq, highlighting where their information and evidence had been included.

To clarify their thinking further they used the following 'challenge' questions:

- Has Darren made as much progress in his first month as we would expect?
- If not, why not?

- If so, what has been the most significant change?
- From our conversations with his parents, what do they think about his progress to date?
- In what ways have we contributed to this view being realistic, given Darren's age and previous development?
- In what ways have we increased Jackie and Tariq's confidence in understanding Darren's development?
- Why has he not made more progress?
- What more could we have done to help him make more progress?
- Are there particular experiences or opportunities that are new to him and could be offered more?

As both Mandy and Jamila were going to attend the meeting with parents they talked through their different roles, agreeing that:

- Mandy would lead the discussions, highlighting the contributions Jackie and Tariq had made to her understanding of Darren
- Jamila would focus on understanding Jackie and Tariq's experiences of the setting, specifically their views about:
  - The welcome and settling in process
  - Communication systems, incidental, daily, weekly, and emergency contact
  - Their aspirations for Darren

Jamila would take notes, summarizing the key points of agreement. The practical arrangements were then made including:

- Dates and times for a meeting
- Arrangements to look after Darren during the discussions
- Booking the room, allowing time for checking furniture, cleanliness, tidiness, and availability of refreshments
- Making a list of information to gather including: Darren's Learning Journal, his favourite activity, video clips, A Prime Areas overview sheet, and the *Development Matters* document.

Mandy had explained to Jackie and Tariq about the meeting and that Jamila, whom they regularly saw at the setting, would be there to help answer any of their questions. In the days leading up to the meeting Mandy made a special point of talking with Jackie and Tariq about specific examples of Darren's development in the three Prime Areas and listened carefully to their similar examples from home.

Putting the SEND Code into practice

This process of preparing for a meeting with parents is useful in supervision, not least to increase the confidence of the practitioner leading the discussion. Explaining your thinking to a colleague requires saying your thoughts out loud and articulating your reasoning. This allows consideration of how these may look and sound from the parent's perspective. This preparation also helped Jamila identify any support or training for Mandy. The 'challenge' questions were a standard part of preparation for a review meeting and allowed consideration of current practice and recording systems with an emphasis on improvement rather than finding fault.

As stated in the SEND Code of Practice 'Parents' early observations of their child are crucial (DfE 2014a: 70). So the preparation also highlighted how conversations with parents to date had contributed to the practitioner's understanding of Darren. There should be no surprises for parents in review discussions. Daily, weekly, monthly, half termly, termly and annual discussions should form a coherent story that is clearly contributed to by the parents themselves (DfE 2014a: 73).

Learning Points

- Detailed preparation is essential for a successful and useful review meeting
- Linking this preparation to supervision provides an opportunity for improving individual and setting practice
- Review meetings must be one element of a coherent discourse with parents

---

Things to think about

- What are the possible benefits and challenges of the SENCO attending regular review meetings for all children?
- In what ways do you use supervision discussions to prepare for planned discussions with parents?
- In what ways does the support you have provided for an individual child represent a 'graduated response' to their level of need and how does this reflect adults' increasing concern?

Collaboration and communication with parents

The Prime Areas of Learning are often the most familiar and easiest for parents to recognize in their child's development. Seeing how their child increases in ability and confidence in moving around, making social connections, using sounds and communicating is fascinating for most parents. However, this does not necessarily mean that discussions about children's progress will be straightforward.

Running a meeting is a specific skill and a useful focus for professional development (see Appendix 1 for a helpful prompt sheet). Effective review meetings demonstrate genuine engagement. Case study 6:2 illustrates:

- continuity between everyday interactions and those in the review meeting
- joint observations with parents
- valuing parents' specialist knowledge
- using *Development Matters* (Early Education 2012) to support discussions about progress

---

Case study 6:2 Darren's first review meeting

Reviewing progress, Darren 10 months old

Having welcomed Darren's parents to the setting, shown them to the meeting room and offered refreshments, Mandy helped to engage Darren in his favourite treasure basket activity. She explained to Jackie that the basket of everyday objects, such as measuring spoons, jar lids and hand bells, really held Darren's interest. Jackie confirmed Mandy's view that his facial expression and body language were demonstrating real pleasure and enjoyment. Responding to Jackie's interest she indicated to her when Darren was reaching and selecting particular objects, putting them to his mouth and looking at them closely before dropping them. Together Jackie and Mandy reflected on how easy it is to take these complex coordinated movements and sensory experiences for granted. Jackie also recollected that these responses were quite recent developments for Darren.

Mandy explained what would happen in the meeting and when it was expected to finish. Although Jackie and Tariq were familiar with Darren's Learning Journal, Mandy demonstrated how it linked to other record-keeping and reminded them that their own observations had been included. She gave everyone a copy of the following summary of Darren's progress:

Physical development

Darren is able to sit, supported by cushions and will play with items that interest him if they are within arm's reach. He likes lying down when Mandy helps him roll over. During nappy changing he sometimes lifts both legs and giggles looking at his feet. At home he will reach for his feet when lying on his back when Jackie plays a 'catch your toes' game with him.

Communication and language

Darren smiles and giggles when Jackie or Tariq talk to him. He recognizes Mandy's voice and looks towards her when she greets him as he arrives at nursery.

Personal, social and emotional development

Darren enjoys being cuddled by Jackie, Tariq and his Gran. He shows his pleasure by snuggling in and gurgling happily. In nursery he is happy to sit on Mandy's knee for a cuddle, especially when he has just woken up after his nap.

Following discussions about Darren's progress in each of the Prime Areas, Mandy confirmed everyone's agreement that the narrative reflected Darren's current development. She and Jamila introduced the *Development Matters* document and discussed how it supported their planning. They then explained the purpose of the overview sheet listening carefully to Jackie and Tariq's comments about Darren's progress in relation to the age bands and descriptions of 'typical' development. Everyone agreed that the description in the Birth to 11 age band was an accurate picture of his development. As he was 10 months old this indicated his progress was in line with typical development. Mandy and Jamila also used the document to highlight what they might see Darren doing next. In particular, that he would soon be crawling and holding onto furniture to pull himself up. Discussions with his parents revealed Darren had not yet tried this. Mandy explained she was surprised that he still relied on support from cushions when sitting up. She suggested planning physical activities he enjoyed that particularly encouraged movement to a sitting position. Jackie agreed that she expected him to be sitting up on his own soon too. She said that she was seeing the health visitor the following week about immunizations and would ask her opinion too. Mandy and Jamila agreed this was a good idea and encouraged Jackie to remind the health visitor that she was welcome to visit or contact the setting to talk further.

Putting the SEND Code into practice

The Prime Areas of Learning provided a clear structure for exploring Darren's developmental progress and building his parents' and practitioners' knowledge of him. It is important to keep in mind how the Prime Areas impact on each other. The areas of need outlined in the SEND Code of Practice help us to think about this inter-relatedness as well as the individuality of each child's needs. The broad areas are:

- Communication and interaction
- Cognition and learning
- Social, emotional and mental health
- Sensory and/or physical needs

(DfE 2014a: 74, 86)

Darren's emerging needs at this stage centre on his physical development. Although this was a 'formal' meeting Mandy's interactions were clearly in keeping with her day-to-day conversations with Jackie and Tariq. Her manner, tone and skill in developing the conversation with Jackie about the treasure baskets demonstrated a genuine shared interest in Darren's responses. The review was notably a two-way process, Jackie offering her specialist knowledge of her son and Mandy her understanding of child development in interpreting their observations.

Learning Points

- A common understanding is being developed, with parents, Key Person and SENCO contributing examples, views and perceptions of Darren's development
- Realistic expectations of Darren are being encouraged through discussion and reference to typical development
- Celebration of success, exploration of doubts and concerns are a natural part of discussions. Everyone is listened to and their views considered carefully

---

Things to think about

- How does your most recent experience of a review meeting compare with this example?
- What challenges might be presented by using *Development Matters* (Early Education 2012) as a focus for discussion about children's progress?
- In what ways do you ensure that your more frequent informal conversations are consistent with discussions in more formal review discussions?

Day-to-day practice continues

Following the review meeting, daily conversations continued including specific references to the review discussions. Jackie found the treasure basket activity easy to provide at home and enjoyed interacting with Darren. Nappy changing and other routines were used to encourage Darren to sit up. Jackie's conversation with the health visitor confirmed Darren was progressing in line with typical development.

Case study 6:3 illustrates:

- early identification of special educational needs
- discussion of mounting concern with parents
- early interventions tailored to an individual child's needs
- using play plans to summarize assessments, plan 'next steps', agree actions and review impact of interventions
- accessing external advice including understanding the relevant 'local offer' published by the local authority

---

Case study 6:3 Darren's review meeting: 12 months

Early identification of Darren's needs

Discussion focused on Darren's current progress in the three Prime Areas to allow comparison with the previous review discussion. These were as follows:

Physical development

Darren had been enjoying the increased opportunity for moving on his tummy and playing with the treasure baskets at home and in the setting. He would hold objects to his mouth and let them go when his interest moved to a new object. Opportunities for moving in the outdoor space had been especially motivating for Darren recently.

Communication and language

Darren had been showing an interest when there was singing or music both at home and in the setting. He particularly seemed to like 'Twinkle, Twinkle Little Star' when Jackie sang it for him.

Personal, social and emotional development

Darren continued to enjoy cuddles with his special people and shows a preference for Mandy to cuddle him if he was upset at nursery, snuggling in and relaxing as she held him.

Everyone felt that Darren had made progress and was engaging in a wider range of activities than previously. They also agreed that, as before his development was best described using the Birth to 11 age band in *Development Matters*. Mandy highlighted the previous expectation that Darren would soon be moving more independently and pulling himself up. Mandy and Jamila were surprised there had not been more progress. His parents agreed but repeated that the health visitor had not been concerned. Jamila talked about the importance of seeing the assessments in context, agreeing that the health visitor was correct about Darren's progress being within the typical range of physical development, as indicated in *Development Matters*. However, it was pointed out that his parents and the practitioners in the setting spent more time with him in a range of situations and that their collective experience of him had been of surprise that he had still not attempted to sit up, or pull himself up. Mandy explained that she was keen to make sure that everything possible was being done to help him. She talked about the purpose of a play plan (see Appendix 4) to evidence more detailed next steps, support and impact on progress. Together they noted Darren's preferred activities. When they were completing the 'Actions' box at the bottom of the form Jamila suggested seeking more specialist advice from the team at the Children's Centre. Tariq, while appreciative of the offer, explained that he felt Darren would develop at his own pace. Mandy agreed, but suggested Jackie or Tariq could be with her when she contacted the team. Mandy retold her previous positive experience of contacting the specialist team, and their helpful advice. Tariq, although not convinced, suggested making the call in the future. Mandy agreed this was a good idea, adding a date to the play plan, when they would have made a joint decision to make the call. Jamila also offered to ask colleagues at the SENCO Network meeting for suggested activities that would support Darren's development. She assured both parents that no names or identifiable details would be given.

Putting the SEND Code into practice

In the review meeting the practitioners expressed their worries about Darren's progress in the Prime Areas. However, even though all adults were concerned, agreement for involving other professionals seemed, for Tariq, at least like a big step. Giving him more time to make the decision was an insightful response showing empathy and understanding. Identifying a specific timescale, recorded on the play plan, was also important in keeping Darren's needs central to the process (DfE 2014a: 8). The play plans also offered clarity about what actions were to be taken, the responsibilities of all involved and relevant timescales. This provided evidence of decisions and how new understanding of Darren's development informed the chosen strategies and approaches. The play plans and review meeting notes should give precise information about progress and evidence of practitioners' 'best endeavours' to support (DfE 2014a: 14).

Learning Points

- Professionals seeing children in different contexts are quite likely to make different judgements since their experience of the child is different. Gathering evidence from a range of perspectives is important to inform secure assessments. Explaining why views differ should be an integral part of the process of reaching conclusions
- Opinions of external professionals are valued, since neither practitioners nor parents are expected to have all the answers or always to be 'right'
- For parents, the act of involving other professionals may seem like a leap into the unknown and can raise anxieties about a child's future progress

Things to think about

- What are the support networks in your local area offering advice and support for SENCOs and Key Persons working with children with SEN?
- What arrangements or opportunities have you identified with your local Health Visiting Team which may support parents in their understanding of child development?
- If you were unhappy about another professional's advice to parents, what action would you take?

Rapid development

Rapid development, particularly of the brain, in the first two years of life, make this period an exciting and dramatic time when skills, abilities and relationships are developing. However, it is also a very vulnerable time when development can be impacted in a range of ways that may have long-term consequences (Oates et al. 2012: 50). The process of building a brain continues throughout life as experiences influence neural connections and pathways resulting in learning taking place. The opportunities for learning and relationships in early exploration set up a complex web of interactions between the cognitive, sensory, physical and emotional systems in our brains and bodies. In this process, attitudes, motivations, and our sense of self inform our approach and engagement with learning opportunities (Ward 2012: 265).

Characteristics of effective learning

The EYFS identifies three 'characteristics of effective learning' and 'practitioners must reflect on the different ways that children learn and reflect these in their practice' (DfE 2014: 9). The characteristics of effective learning help us to understand the importance of 'how' children learn rather than simply focusing on 'what' they learn (Stewart 2011: 8). These characteristics are:

1 *Playing and exploring* – children investigate and experience things, and 'have a go'
2 *Active learning* – children concentrate and keep on trying if they encounter difficulties, and enjoy achievements

3   *Creating and thinking critically* – children have and develop their own ideas, make links between ideas, and develop strategies for doing things

Using the characteristics of effective learning

Darren's approach to learning is increasingly being understood by practitioners and parents. They talk about their observations and consider how these relate to the characteristics of effective learning.

Case study 6:4 illustrates:

- interpretations of observations which highlight increasing adult understanding of Darren's learning characteristics
- recognizing continuity and consistency in Darren's approaches to activities and situations
- how the characteristics of effective learning are demonstrated across a range of areas of learning

---

Case study 6:4 Darren's characteristics of effective learning

Understanding how Darren learns

1. Play and exploration

Finding out and exploring

Much of Darren's early learning was connected with demonstrating his drive to explore and play with new objects, in order to find out what they were and what they could do. Particular examples which were noted included using treasure baskets, rolling different sized balls, popping bubbles and playing peek-a-boo led by an adult.

Playing with what they know

As practitioners compared observations they realized that Darren was also playing with ideas in other ways. For example, he began rolling a ball with another child and leading a peek-a-boo game with his Key Person.

Willing to have a go

Once Darren's physical strength and movement developed, he demonstrated a real enthusiasm to have a go at new things and to get involved. This was demonstrated in his early involvement in playing chase with other children, jumping off the balance bar and balancing on the 'big trucks'.

2. Active learning

Being involved and concentrating
The challenges Darren faced in developing his strength and coordination particularly for fine motor activities showed his ability to maintain his attention on a specific task, for example, when posting coins in a money box, in threading activities and when using scissors.

Keeping on trying
As with the fine motor activities Darren needed time to build his strength and coordination for independent movement. His perseverance and determination were particularly noticeable when he was pulling himself up to standing, crawling upstairs, building and knocking down brick towers, moving towards and engaging with a wider variety of activities.

This persistence and ability to come back from disappointments also showed in his making and sustaining of relationships with other children.

Enjoying achieving what they set out to do
From early on in Darren's time in the toddler room his pleasure in his own successes was obvious. This was particularly evident when he was able to pull himself up to standing independently, cruise round the furniture, pour drinks for other children and feed himself.

3. Creating and thinking critically

Having their own ideas
As Darren became more interested in Expressive Arts and Design and exploring materials, he began selecting different paper, shapes, objects and textures to make his pictures and models. He demonstrated using his own ideas in finding different ways to combine the large blocks and crates to make a den.

When he interacted with others and communicated his emotions Darren also began to find alternative ways of dealing with frustrations. In particular, rather than hitting out, he began vocalizing his feelings making his 'cross noise' alerting practitioners and other children that he was feeling frustrated.

Making links
Darren frequently surprised practitioners by being able to anticipate and predict what came next in familiar action rhymes. Once he was able to match numbers with objects he began making links with the numbers seen in the setting, at home and when he was on outings.

Choosing ways to do things
When Darren wanted to communicate that he had enjoyed something, he chose to use a combination of signs, symbols and pictures, but when he wanted to communicate his immediate needs he used the Makaton signs for 'more', 'toilet', 'drink' and 'biscuit' – these were the signs he had first learned and used most confidently.

In his quest to build taller and taller towers Darren chose both where to build, and which sets of blocks to use. When pouring drinks for other children, Darren changed the order of pouring to make it easier to hold the jug and pour accurately.

Putting the SEND Code into practice

Darren is demonstrating his curiosity about the world around him but also actively engaging in challenging situations and thoughtful approaches to overcome problems. The conscious adjustment to the order of pouring drinks gives a real insight into how, given the opportunity, Darren is able to construct a solution and persevere to achieve his goal. This attention to the detail of how Darren learns helps to show the inter-relatedness of the Prime Areas, particularly communication and language with physical development, acknowledging his strengths as well as his challenges (DfE 2014a: 74, 75).

Learning Points

- Understanding Darren's characteristics as a learner enabled practitioners to successfully support his learning
- Collaborating and reflecting on observations led to a deeper understanding of Darren's strengths
- For Darren to develop his communication with others, practitioners encouraged him to use a combination of approaches personal to him

Things to think about

- In what ways has your knowledge of the characteristics of effective learning helped you to understand a child's strengths recently?
- What are the advantages of including the characteristics of effective learning as a focus of discussion with parents?
- How would you describe your own characteristics of effective learning?

Involving external services

Engaging external services needs to be carefully coordinated with parents included at every stage. Jackie and Tariq finally made the call with Mandy, to the Early Years team at the Children's Centre. They were relieved when this resulted in having an opportunity to talk with a physiotherapist who provided some suggestions for strengthening Darren's muscles. She also asked if Mandy could email her three weeks later with an update about Darren's progress. His parents were delighted with the suggested activities and felt confident about using them at home.

This case study illustrates:

- ways to engage positively with external services
- the importance of communicating information about current progress and concerns
- effectively supporting parents with their first engagement with an external service can lead to subsequent referrals or contact being approached more confidently

Case study 6:5 Darren's progress from 13 to 25 months

Review meetings provide coherent communication

At the next meeting everyone was delighted that Darren had made progress towards sitting up on his own. Mandy, Jackie and Tariq updated the play plan and summary of the Prime Areas to show Darren's progress, and emailed it to the physiotherapist. Given this information, the physiotherapist contacted Jackie and Tariq suggesting a referral so she could meet Darren to devise some new activities. They happily agreed and the referral was made through the Disability Link Worker who was based at the Children's Centre, whose role it is to coordinate SEND support for the EYFS settings in the immediate locality.

Monitoring progress

Monthly review meetings continued and play plans were updated with contributions from the physiotherapist. By the time Darren was 20 months old, Mandy and Jamila were raising further concerns about his communication and language (see progress tracking in Appendix 3). All adults agreed that whilst his understanding was within the range of typical development, his speech did not seem to be progressing well. Mandy had concerns that this could also impact on his relationships with other children. Following their previous positive experience Jackie and

Tariq agreed to contact the Disability Link Worker for advice. A referral to the Speech and Language Therapy Team was made and advice and suggestions provided.

Following input from the Speech and Language Therapist Mandy focused on using songs and puppets as suggested to encourage Darren's spoken language. Makaton sign language, designed to support children's early development of verbal language, had also been recommended, and Mandy had introduced signs for 'more' and 'finish' and had also been helping Darren to join in action rhymes with the other children in her Key Group. Darren was now babbling, copying mouth movements and facial expressions.

However, ongoing concerns about Darren's progress led Jackie and Tariq to agree the following actions:

- to provide details to the setting of their family doctor
- for Mandy to collate all relevant information
- to compile a letter outlining concerns, details of interventions and progress to date
- The Disability Link Worker to complete a Common Assessment Framework (CAF) form with them

The purpose of the CAF (or Early Help assessment) was, first, to provide a holistic view of Darren's needs as well as those of his family, and, second, to ensure multi-agency involvement was regularly reviewed and information communicated appropriately. Darren would soon be due for his two-year progress check, which would summarize his development in the Prime Areas. As part of the Healthy Child Programme, a health check, as detailed in the child's Personal Health Record, would also be carried out at around 30 months old. Therefore the local health visiting team were contacted and invited to attend the next review discussion.

Outcomes

After a referral from the family doctor Darren had an appointment with a paediatrician, and following a range of assessments, he was diagnosed with a rare genetic disorder. The impact of the disorder was likely to result in developmental delay but it was unclear how extensive this might be. For his parents this news gave rise to very mixed feelings. They were relieved to have a reason for Darren's atypical patterns of progress and to know the name of this since they believed this information might help them to access services when necessary. However, they were anxious about Darren's future and the possible extent of his difficulties as he matured. Mandy and Jamila had many discussions about the diagnosis and its implications. They used the evidence they had already gathered about Darren's progress to reassure his parents that he was making progress, particularly in his understanding of language. The Disability Link Worker was available to talk frequently with parents and liaise with the setting, ensuring that information was consistent.

Putting the SEND Code into practice

In this case study the practitioners demonstrated the importance of listening carefully to parents. Having been supported in their first contact with the physiotherapist, Tariq and Jackie demonstrated increasing confidence in working in partnership. Mandy and Jamila realized the importance of everyone having up-to-date and relevant information about Darren's progress to inform their judgements and suggestions. This also ensured that Jackie and Tariq had the information they needed to make appropriate decisions about support for Darren (DfE 2014a: 68). Mandy and Jamila were also sensitive in their understanding of other professionals and offered a variety of ways to include them in the process such as:

1   sending an update on Darren's progress enabling each professional to have feedback on his development
2   offering an opportunity to provide suggestions which would help to inform future support
3   allowing time to reflect on the success of previous strategies
4   following up with notes from the meeting, continuing the engagement, and communicating current priorities for his support

Learning Points

- The information provided by EY practitioners should be clear and detailed so that parents can use it to support their communication with other professionals giving evidence of the impact of interventions as well as rates and patterns of progress
- Parents' attitudes about seeking advice beyond the setting is likely to be different from that of practitioners, especially on the first occasion
- Keeping the child at the centre of our thinking helps to emphasize the common purpose between services

---

Things to think about

- What happens once a CAF/Early Help form has been completed in your local area at the moment?
- What discussions have you had with your local health visitor team about the two-year progress checks?
- In what ways do you support families to engage positively with different professionals when appropriate?

Prime Areas of Learning and the early identification of SEN

This chapter has focused on the early identification of Darren's specific needs. The case studies show how his Key Person, employing the setting's recording systems, identified an unusual pattern in his progress in the three Prime Areas. This was in line with her professional perception that his physical development was inconsistent with his language and personal, social and emotional progress. Crucially she sought out his parents' perceptions at this early stage ensuring there was no delay in making provision for Darren (DfE 2014: 75).

When the practitioners first met Darren and his parents there was no way of knowing that he had special educational needs, nor that links with other agencies would be needed to support his development. Therefore, the systems and practices to establish positive relationships with all parents need to be robust yet flexible enough to support this eventuality.

The discussions where practitioners highlight concerns are rarely easy, they need to be thought about carefully and planned for in every detail. However, the quality and content of all interactions with parents influence these conversations. Parents and practitioners inevitably see different aspects of a child's development and it is only by bringing these together that we can fully understand the child's progress and the challenges they may face in reaching milestones.

As professionals we gradually build a picture through observation, discussion and reflection about a child's development, learning and progress. It is only by taking parents with us on this journey, rather than presenting them with conclusions, that we will really support the child and their family.

Improving and developing practice

To what extent are these statements true for your setting?

- The Prime Areas of Learning are recognized as a key indicator of a child's overall progress and are understood to be inter-related.
- Practitioners' everyday record-keeping makes a significant contribution to the early identification of SEN.
- 'Early Intervention' is understood to be about tailoring 'next steps' very clearly to a child's needs based on all the available knowledge of a child at home and in the setting.
- Parents are understood to have specialist knowledge about their child which can be linked with practitioners' perspectives.
- All parents are actively involved in all discussions and consideration of their child's progress and support needs.

Key Points

- The 'assess, plan, do, review' cycle from the SEND Code of Practice (DfE 2014a) aligns easily with the EYFS observation, assessment and planning cycle used for all children. Along with a robust tracking system this creates a coherent system for early identification and intervention. Knowledge of patterns and rates of progress can provide an early warning system for identifying a child's needs but can also provide evidence of the effectiveness of any strategies and interventions undertaken. Moderating decisions about a child's development and learning and devising intervention strategies can be effectively supported through supervision sessions where ideas can be explored with colleagues.
- The local offer, published by the local authority, provides an important source of relevant information about special educational needs provision. Making contact with practitioners from external services, and sharing expertise and understanding of roles is useful professional development for everyone. It also helps to know what response parents can expect if a referral or appointment is made.

- Particularly at times of transition or assessment, multi-agency involvement in review meetings is an effective way of collating information, with parents taking a leading role in the decision-making. The right information needs to be available in an easily accessible format to inform everyone's thinking. This is likely to include summaries of key points as well as original evidence such as learning journals. Running such a meeting requires a set of skills that should be developed as part of professional development.

PART 3
Making the difference

7   The practitioner's perspective

Chapter themes

- The importance of articulating our practice and recognizing a common purpose across services

- The role of the SENCO as a leader and facilitator, demonstrating advocacy, mediation and solution-focused problem-solving

- The Key Person as a knowledgeable observer and advocate who is loving and responsive, tuning into each child's communication

As we saw in Part 1, the intended purpose of provision for young children and those with special educational needs has changed over time. This has included:

- looking after children to enable parents to work
- improving life chances
- preparing for employment
- making a positive impact on an individual's well-being

The lack of a common understanding about what we are setting out to do often can lead to diluted impact. Margaret Hodge, reflecting on her role as former MP and Children's Minister, suggested that although much had been achieved in recent decades, clarity about the purpose of childcare would have increased the impact of policy initiatives. She indicated a number of competing priorities:

- giving children a good start in life
- nurture
- education

- equality of opportunity
- getting parents back to work
- reducing the welfare budget

Furthermore these competing priorities had not provided a clear focus on the child as the central priority (Gaunt 2014).

The SEND Code of Practice expresses its purpose as helping children and young people 'achieve the best possible educational and other outcomes, preparing them effectively for adulthood' (DfE 2014a: 8). From September 2014 each Local Authority is required, under the Children and Families Act 2014, to publish how they will achieve this purpose. This 'local offer' must set out the education, health and social care provision available. By directly involving those with special educational needs in regularly reviewing the local offer, the intention is that provision will also become increasingly responsive to local need (DfE 2014a: 48). Recent research, commissioned by local authorities, identified the following as helping families to engage with services:

- availability of information about what is on offer
- simple, easy to understand access routes
- family/friend support to access services
- previous positive experience of services
- positive perceptions of what the service does
- collaboration between services to coordinate support

(Easton et al. 2013: 37)

Similarly, at the heart of EYFS is the principle of positive relationships and all practitioners are expected to work collaboratively to meet an individual child's needs (DfE 2014: 1). The single factor that 'oils the wheels' and makes these relationships work is the attitude of leaders and of individual practitioners. Such people demonstrate a 'can do' approach and recognize that listening carefully to families and children will also inform improvements to their provision.

Early years practitioners are often involved in initial conversations with parents about accessing external support for children. How practitioners describe the support available will impact on parental expectations. Anticipating a welcoming response can reduce anxiety and defensiveness as new relationships are established. Practitioner knowledge of the local offer will inform such conversations with parents.

The following case studies offer some insights into local provision from the perspective of the practitioners working in them. The five case studies explore the following contexts:

- health assessment and diagnosis process for Autistic Spectrum Disorder (ASD)

- outreach support for children with SEN and disabilities
- cohesive SEN provision in a primary school
- approaches to inclusion in a maintained nursery school
- approaches to inclusion in a private nursery school

The joint working between health, education and social care, a fundamental part of the SEND Code of Practice is a 'work in progress' in the majority of local authorities and different pathways to support exist in each geographical area. Understanding how other services work and what might be experienced at an appointment can enable practitioners to help a parent to feel more confident about a referral being made.

Case study 7:1 gives an example of how pathways to support work in one city-based health authority. In particular, this case study illustrates:

- a single point of referral
- collaborative working to gain a holistic view of the child
- timely feedback to parents and practitioners after multi-agency assessments

---

Case study 7:1 Collaboration and responsive pathways to support

Health assessment and diagnosis process for Autistic Spectrum Disorder

The co-location of related services at the Child Development Centre encourages close liaison between teams. A single point of referral reduces bureaucracy and waiting times, allowing different health professionals to see a child after initial referral. All health professionals are encouraged to suggest improvements to responsiveness and efficiency of services.

Pathways

School SENCOs can contact educational psychologists and speech therapists directly and, via the school nurse, have access to pediatricians or General Practitioners (GPs). Early years practitioners can support parents in contacting their health visitor or GP to refer to any health specialists. They can also signpost parents to the twice-weekly speech therapy 'drop-in' clinic and, with parental consent phone pediatricians directly for advice.

Working together

With parental consent, health professionals contact early years settings for information about the child's development and progress. This valued information offers a more holistic view of the child than that available from clinic visits. In ASD/Developmental Delay Assessments the educational psychologist and speech and language therapist will observe the child in their setting. Health visitors, speech therapists and educational psychologists are increasingly involved with Children's Centres, running on-site clinics and attending sessions with parents.

Diagnostic process: Autistic Spectrum Disorder

The Multi-Disciplinary Team (pre-school) is the core assessment team, it includes an educational psychologist, a speech and language therapist and a paediatrician. Referrals come from health visitors, GPs, school nurses, speech therapists, paediatricians and other health professionals. Referrals are discussed at regular meetings and if appropriate allocated to a Consultant Paediatrician for follow-up investigations. Outcomes of assessments are communciated at the Social Communication Difficulty Multi-Disciplinary Team (SCD) pre-school meeting. A dedicated coordinator with access to professionals' timetables organizes these meetings.

The format of the SCD meeting is:

- professionals communicate the outcomes of assessments directly to parents
- they make a strategy agreement with early years setting practitioners and health visitors
- a summary report and plan are sent out to all parties
- an information pack about the support plan and local services is given to parents at the meeting

Provision for children with autism and the relevant diagnostic process are constantly under review through the Autistic Spectrum Disorder (ASD) coordinating meeting. This involves paediatricians, therapists, SENCOs, headteachers and Designated Nursery Leaders. In addition, the ASD partnership board, including parent and practitioner representatives, oversees the development of services for children with Autistic Spectrum Disorder, including offering effective information sharing.

Putting the SEND Code into practice

All services evolve over time and are subject to policy changes but clarity of purpose and approach increases the continuity of experience for children and their families. The single point of referral in this case simplifies the process for families and encourages more flexible working between teams involved in the service. Gathering information from home and early years provision also increases the chance of appropriate early intervention and timely support.

Most diagnostic processes are complex and require multi-agency involvement; autistic spectrum disorder (ASD) is a case in point. Coordinating the assessments and diagnosis process with parents in mind will strongly influence how the diagnosis is received and their attitudes to seeking further help. In this case study, professional time is used to maximum benefit allowing for a multi-agency discussion as well as clear and prompt feedback to parents. Having direct contact between parents and professionals reduces the likelihood of misunderstandings and establishes relationships with the common purpose of meeting the child's individual needs.

Learning Points

- Having a clear common purpose helps to break down barriers between those with different responsibilities
- Facilitating a holistic view of the child's life increases the effectiveness of support
- Engaging those receiving the service in the review process increases responsiveness

Things to think about

- In what ways do early years practitioners in your area currently contribute to diagnostic processes, for example, for ASD?
- What mechanisms are there for feedback to specific services to increase their responsiveness to the needs of children and families?
- Which is the most responsive and easily accessed service in your area for children with special educational needs? What makes it work so well? In what ways can you give them feedback about their success?

Outreach support

In Case study 7:2 the idea of clarity of purpose includes a model of working which underpins all aspects of the team's work. This has the benefit of maintaining continuity beyond individual personalities. Team members may come and go but the approach of the service is familiar and predictable in its structure.

The service approach is based on the Family Partnership Model, which identifies the characteristics of effective partnership as:

- working together with active participation/involvement
- developing and maintaining genuine connectedness
- distributing decision-making power
- recognizing complementary expertise and roles
- sharing and agreeing aims and the process of helping
- negotiation of disagreement
- showing mutual trust and respect
- developing and maintaining openness and honesty
- communicating clearly

(Davis and Day 2007: 3)

The team works to establish this partnership relationship with each family and to respond to parental priorities. The ultimate goal is for families to gain confidence and recognize their own resourcefulness. This approach is intended to increase resilience and reduce the need for repeated similar forms of support.

This case study illustrates that:

- listening carefully to parents' priorities underpins the partnership work
- supervision enables moderation of decisions and adherence to the Family Partnership Model
- this model of working facilitates responsive and flexible support for families

---

Case study 7:2 Family Partnership Model for outreach support

Outreach support for children with SEN and disabilities

Referrals come from a range of practitioners who present their cases to the local authority Funding Panel. A high percentage of referrals are for children with Autistic Spectrum Disorder. This team currently has nine practitioners, each of whom has weekly supervision with the Team Leader.

The usual practice is to see children (with parental permission) in their EYFS settings and engage with practitioners. The purpose of this is to highlight the child's strengths which contributes to a holistic understanding of their needs. Relationships between parents and EYFS practitioners are supported to encourage a collaborative development of strategies to support the child.

Responsiveness

Programme sessions are used flexibly, informed by parental priorities, for example, to target particular times of day such as mealtimes or bedtimes. Parents report that this responsiveness means they feel really listened to and valued. Another example is of a group of parents who explained their frustrations about constantly explaining their children's behaviour during park visits. They described their wish for their children to be able to play in the local park where the majority of adults understood their behaviour. In response, the team with a National Autistic Society colleague, supported parents to organize 'play-dates' at a local park which allowed team members and parents to engage with the children and their friends in an atmosphere of acceptance with no need to explain the idiosyncrasies of their child's behaviour.

Putting the SEND Code into practice

The use of the Family Partnership Model not only helps communicate the purpose of this service but provides continuity in decision-making and family experience. Using supervision, the team leader also implements the characteristics of effective partnership to support the professional development of the team. Members of the team are guided, encouraged and supported to acquire skills and confidence as well as recognize their own specific strengths as they support particular families.

Learning Points

- Any model of working needs to be maintained and applied consistently to be effective
- Supervision is an important tool for leaders to guide decision-making and facilitate staff development
- The clear articulation of the purpose of a service helps to ensure the realistic expectations of those using it

Things to think about

- How would you articulate the purpose of your setting?
- In what ways does your experience of supervision help to guide your decision-making towards achieving this purpose?
- In what ways has your setting demonstrated responsiveness to children's and/or parents' needs in the last six months?

Maintained primary school

The SEND Code of Practice (DfE 2014a: 95) requires maintained sector schools, including nursery schools, to publish their SEN information report explaining how they identify and support children with special educational needs. Individual schools will have evolved systems and processes with many common features but with interventions that are tailored to meet the needs of their current population. The extent to which particular schools seem able to welcome and adapt to meet the needs of individual children and their families varies considerably. For parents, the SEN information report for a school will be useful in making comparisons between different settings and provision.

Case study 7:3 shows how meeting the needs of each individual child has led to flexible and comprehensive provision in a primary school. Starting from the EYFS concept of the 'Unique Child', parents and staff together review evidence of a child's development and learning, assessing how best to support future progress. Interventions have been carefully selected, informed by staff research beyond the setting. This case study illustrates:

- a range of interventions that complement each other in supporting children and their families
- decision-making at the lowest appropriate level in the organization linked with accountability and responsibility for impact
- continuity of an inclusive approach to child and adult learning

Case study 7:3 Inclusive approaches in the primary school

Cohesive SEN provision in the primary school

This school has a very proactive approach to inclusion, using a range of interventions to support children's individual needs including: Place2be counselling provision (www.place2be.org.uk) 2.5 days per week which is targeted at those with less severe needs. This is seen as integral to the school. It also provides staff training on relevant topics such as attachment. Annual targets are set for the programme which is reviewed by governors, and include impact on children's progress, as demonstrated through individual case studies. Evidence shows that fewer children in the upper school require support than did prior to the programme being implemented. This is complemented by the adaptability of routines across the school such as use of the ICT suite to support children during lunchtime or as appropriate. Recognizing that children's behaviour is a means of communication underpins the school's approach to behavioural concerns. The priority is to give each child the 'best possible chance' to succeed. All children's learning about behaviour and expectations is explicitly supported during an 'establishment phase' (Rogers and McPherson 2008: 9) in the autumn term. All adults apply a 'de-escalating' approach to children's emotional and behavioural responses. Colleagues work collaboratively to enable 'the adult who understands this child best' to be available when necessary or appropriate.

The Learning Zone (Year 1 upwards) is based on nurture group principles and uses the Boxall Profile (Bennathan and Boxall 1998) to assess and monitor progress. The focus of the group is PSED but with a differentiated academic curriculum, emphasizing speech and language and including a range of activities such as cooking and ICT. Weekly team supervision discussions are used to explore concerns, monitor progress and identify any staff training needs. Parents are very supportive of this provision in the school.

Staff training

Professional development is encouraged, for example, places on the City and Guilds 'Specialist Leaders of Behaviour and Attendance' course are funded by the school. Local courses related to dyslexia and speech and language development are funded and staff are supported to pursue particular areas of interest. Visits to local specialist provision form part of regular training day agendas. All staff model a facilitative approach to children's learning as opposed to presenting themselves as the 'font of all knowledge'. The creation of a learning ethos for adults as well as children demonstrates learning itself as something valued in the school community.

Impact of support

The budget for teaching assistant (TA) support is delegated to year group leaders to enable responsive and flexible provision for current children. Leaders are accountable for children making progress. Subject coordinators and the Senior Leadership team monitor progress data carefully. This enables evidence-based professional discussions and a robust early warning system indicating that teaching approaches need amending or that additional support is required. Developing a quality tracking system enabling school, year group, class, pupil grouping as well as individual progress data to be interrogated and compared year on year has been a priority.

The Unique Child

In EYFS the class teacher spends time with parents looking at records from previous provision and devising the settling programme together. Where concerns arise these are discussed with the leadership team. Risk and protective factors are reviewed, ensuring a holistic perspective of the child's current situation and identification of appropriate support.

Putting the SEND Code into practice

This school provision has developed over time, but crucially has grown from a clear purpose to meet individual children's needs. As new interventions are developed and existing ones extended, they are scrutinized to ensure impact and continuity with other support. The tracking of children's progress is the central evidence that allows this to be a robust and effective process. Professional challenge about why children have or have not made progress allows for collaborative problem-solving and an increasing understanding of what works for individual children. This can only work, however, if adults are also encouraged in their learning and increase their skill levels. The success of learning, whether for adult or child, is valued and understood throughout the school.

Learning Points

- A robust tracking progress system allowing interrogation of child-level data is an important tool in understanding and evidencing impact of interventions. This includes:
  - the child's individual progress
  - early identification of special educational needs
  - effectiveness of provision in providing for particular groups (such as boys, girls, those entitled to free school meals, those for whom English is an additional language, and so on)
- Interventions, whether a tailored 'settling-in' process or specific programme such as Place2Be, needs to be 'in tune' with the approaches and purpose of the organization to be successful
- Responsibility and accountability need to be related to specific, challenging but achievable impacts for individual or groups of children

Things to think about

- Currently what 'interventions' might you employ to meet a child's individual needs during their 'settling-in' period?
- Which groups currently represented in your setting are making more progress than similar groups last year? For example, summer-born children, children from particular ethnic groups, or older boys/girls, younger boys/girls
- What similarities are there in the way children and adults are encouraged to learn in your provision?

Maintained nursery school

Case study 7:4 illustrates how the expressed purpose of 'meeting the needs of children and families in the local community' translates into day-to-day practice. In particular, it illustrates:

- creative thinking about how aspects of provision can support each other
- relationships and quality interactions being the core of effective practice
- strong leadership is needed to manage tensions arising from

Case study 7:4 Making our common purpose a daily reality

Approaches to inclusion in a maintained nursery school

The EYFS principle of the Unique Child is at the heart of decision-making, planning and the day-to-day experience of children and adults in this nursery. A range of provision is offered from 8.00am to 6.00pm all year round to meet the needs of all children in the local community. Inclusion is a high priority in planning improvements, adding to existing changing facilities with mobile hoist and the accessibility of outdoor/indoor areas. Staff training is highly valued as a way of increasing the collective under-standing of special educational needs. All staff are involved in training linked to a particular child's special educational needs such as:

- epilepsy
- gastric feeding
- tracheotomy
- specific impairments

Conscious effort is made to maintain a network of contacts in local services and agencies for advice and support.

Collaborative working with parents

Building effective partnerships with parents, though often testing, is seen as a real investment in children's learning. All practitioners strive for a common language and understanding with parents of their child's needs. Although there are children currently attending with high-level, complex needs, no child has 1:1 support allocated and all staff members take responsibility for all children.

The Key Person system

The EYFS Key Person system in this nursery means each Key Person has 18 families in their group. Children with special educational needs are allocated two Key Persons to ensure continuity for the family and collabor-ative decision-making.

The short interactions at the beginning and end of day with parents build on the staff's existing understanding of family priorities, stresses and celebrations, thus developing a professional understanding of the whole family. This provides a context to understand each child's emotions and behaviour.

A particular issue in the nursery school context is that a child may only attend for one academic year. For children with special educational needs this can be problematic and prior to the Children and Families Act (2014) the statutory assessment process dictated the following timescales:

- September to November – IEP's evidencing rate of progress, support and involvement of other agencies
- January – application for statutory assessment submitted to SEN Panel
- March – application for special school place, or support in mainstream
- May – special school places allocation

Inherent in this process was, as discussed in Chapter 6, the danger of focusing on a child's difficulties to demonstrate level of needs and secure future specialist support. Further, in this local authority a perceived shortage of special school places leads parents to feel children are 'in competition' for resources. Intervention from the Educational Psychology Service is also tied to the statutory assessment process rather than available as part of early intervention. It takes strong leadership and staff confidence to continue working to the EYFS principle of seeing each Unique Child as a competent and capable learner in this context.

Putting the SEND Code into practice

Although in the nursery, systems and processes are clearly focused on their purpose of meeting the needs of local children and families, there can be tensions in the wider context at locality, local authority, and national policy level. The importance of strong leadership to manage these competing priorities whilst staying true to the organization's core purpose cannot be over-emphasized.

The priority in this nursery school is to use resources flexibly to meet a child's needs. Parents, particularly those with children who have special educational needs, often have many appointments, forms, and logistical problem-solving to occupy their thoughts, in addition to the daily demands of being a parent. For them, being able to build a relationship with early years practitioners who demonstrate a genuine 'can do' approach to challenges is both a practical and emotional support.

Learning Points

- The purpose, as perceived within early years provision has to be maintained in the face of external tensions such as local authority systems and national policy
- Strong leadership can enable all staff to take appropriate responsibility for individual children, including those with complex special educational needs
- Working collaboratively across agencies, between settings, localities or internally may not be effortless, but can facilitate greater understanding and more flexible, effective support for families

---

Things to think about

- In which aspect of your provision could greater flexibility be introduced to support families' needs?
- Which external systems or processes are currently causing a tension with your understanding of the purpose of your provision?
- Where are your most effective collaborative relationships, how could these be extended?

Conclusion

The continuity of a common purpose in supporting all children has been highlighted in a range of provision throughout the case studies. They have also illustrated situations where individuals are making a positive difference to families' experience of their service.

A significant factor in this continuity is the importance of effective supervision. The opportunity to moderate and rehearse decision-making, maintain common aims and keep the child's needs central, is invaluable to building practitioner confidence and skill. This can only be achieved where professional relationships are nurtured through effective leadership.

The role of the SENCO is crucial in organizing and mobilizing support for individual children, but it is also a leadership role in the setting. As we saw, in the maintained and private nursery schools the SENCOs worked closely with the Key Persons, building confidence in engaging with parents and tuning into each child's communication. Although the focus has been on children with special educational needs, it is evident that this approach is effective practice for all children in the EYFS. The development of such approaches for children with special educational needs will inevitably improve the quality of provision for all children.

Improving and developing practice

- How would you describe the 'common purpose' of the practitioners in your setting? Would your colleagues and parents agree?
- In what ways could supervision be used more effectively in your setting to develop each practitioner's confidence in articulating their practice related to children with special educational needs?
- In what ways are Key Persons encouraged, through supervision, to increase their confidence in working with children with special educational needs and their families?

Key Points

- The EYFS provides a principled approach that supports a common purpose across a range of provision. Being able to articulate this with parents and colleagues from other services helps to establish a common purpose of meeting a child's individual needs.
- EYFS settings are expected to have an identified SENCO as part of their arrangements for meeting children's needs (DfE 2014: 77). The SENCO role is one of leadership, supporting colleagues to fulfil their responsibilities in meeting each child's needs. The SENCO's attitude towards children and parents will be a major contributor to the overall ethos of the setting. The SENCO's engagement with practitioners from other services will also develop greater understanding of the local offer.
- Every child in EYFS has a Key Person to advocate and mediate for them. The Key Person's specialist knowledge of each child's communication and likely response is crucial in early identification of their needs and in effective intervention. The quality of day-to-day conversations with parents can ensure that they have the evidence available to make informed decisions about support for their child.

8 The parents' perspective

Chapter themes

- Listening to parents' perspectives and keeping their views central to decision-making

- Increasing parents' confidence in their own ability to advocate for their child and to engage positively with appropriate services

- Looking for opportunities to be flexible and adaptable, employing our 'best endeavours' and making reasonable adjustments to accommodate children's needs

The special needs journey, although different for every family, has common elements and in listening to individual parents telling their stories it becomes clear that there are particular themes related to early years. The following case studies are included to highlight these and are intended to present a respectful representation of information directly provided by parents.

The Family Partnership Model (Davis and Day 2007) mentioned in Chapter 7, is also fundamental to the Early Support Programme (National Children's Bureau 2013). Skills highlighted for working effectively in partnership with parents are:

- Attention/active listening
- Prompting and exploring
- Empathetic responding
- Summarizing
- Enabling change

- Negotiating
- Problem solving

(Early Support 2006: 4)

Also the following qualities are considered necessary for the person facilitating the help for parents:

- Respect
- Empathy
- Genuineness
- Humility
- Quiet enthusiasm
- Personal integrity
- Professional knowledge

(Early Support 2006: 5)

There are obvious parallels with the positive relationships principle of the EYFS and practitioners in high quality provision would employ these skills and abilities with all parents, not just with those whose children have special educational needs or disabilities.

Typically, during the early years from birth to 5 parents are learning about their child, including implications of any diagnosis or assessments. Alternatively, they may be having their own growing concerns and be alert to that the fact that someone else shares their concerns.

Having a child with special needs is usually both life-changing and highly emotional and takes time to assimilate into an existing understanding of a family's life and relationships. The following case studies give a sense of how this has been experienced by seven families. The experiences of the first three families illustrate the process of early identification during the period when their children attended private nursery settings in a London borough. Hearing about a child's complex needs soon after birth is a very different experience from this later identification. The narratives of the further four families highlight their experiences of multi-agency involvement, EYFS provision, and the statutory assessment process. Finally, the chapter concludes with the words of advice these parents wanted to pass on to others finding themselves in a similar situation.

The case studies illustrate:

- diversity of experience
- the significant impact an individual practitioner can have on the experience of a family of a child with special needs
- the detailed specialist knowledge that parents have about their children

- the parameters of flexible and adaptable support for children and families provided in different settings

Early identification in early years provision: Steven, Josh and Hamsa

Three boys (Steven, Josh and Hamsa) attend the following provision:

- Steven: private nursery and local primary school
- Josh: private nursery and local primary school
- Hamsa: private nursery and specialist provision

Case study 8:1 Steven's transition to reception class in school

Establishing new relationships

Steven's mother, Jane, was very happy with the progress he had made. He now plays with up to three other children and has two special friends. He would be going to school in September, which would be a big change, though once he got to know individual children, she felt he would be fine.

To support the transition the class teacher and Inclusion Coordinator from the school (in an adjoining LA) visited the nursery to meet Steven and his Key Person. Jane visited the school twice with his Key Person from nursery. Going with the Key Person was very supportive and helped to clarify details of successful strategies that would be adopted to support Steven in the transition into school. Jane was concerned that the school was very big, she worried Steven would feel lost and she wanted to be sure that someone would 'look out for him', at least at the start. However, on her visit the staff have been welcoming and supportive, helping her to feel positive about the move.

Jane felt confident about Steven's progress at nursery because the manager listened carefully to her. They both had specific knowledge of Steven and worked together to solve problems and communicate their priorities to other professionals involved.

Case study 8:2 Understanding Josh's needs

Recognizing parents' specialist knowledge

Josh's dad, Lincoln, described major improvements in his son's learning and social connections, after a long and difficult start in life. Josh was diagnosed with autism three years earlier, but Lincoln did not agree with the diagnosis. He felt Josh was too young for such a diagnosis and, in his experience, considered that such labelling hurts more than it is helpful. Lincoln challenged the diagnosis with the paediatrician.

Around this time the family was having many difficulties such that Lincoln was no longer living in the family home and only seeing his son during supervised visits at the local contact centre. The nursery manager was aware of these challenges but, based on evidence gathered, observing Josh's play and interactions, understood that he was really missing seeing his Dad. For example, he would pretend to phone and talk to his Dad, was overjoyed to see him when he met up with him and was very at ease when he was present.

The nursery manager talked with both parents to suggest that supervised contact visits should take place at the nursery which was a more familiar environment for Josh. Following the required checks this arrangement was put in place and worked very well. Lincoln explained, emotionally, that everyone was now working together as a team to help and support Josh. In the nursery, Lincoln demonstrated a real aptitude for working sensitively with Josh as well as other children.

Josh then began attending reception class and Lincoln helps whenever possible. All staff have been very welcoming, working closely with Lincoln to understand Josh and his approach to learning. Over the years Lincoln has worked hard to understand Josh as a person, finding effective ways to help him feel less anxious and support his social connections. Lincoln's aspirations for Josh are that he will be a happy, independent adult, able to access support when he needs it and perhaps able eventually to run his own business.

Currently, the nursery manager is working with Lincoln to explore appropriate training courses so that he can gain childcare qualifications. Lincoln hopes in time to specialize in working with children who have autism.

Case study 8:3 Hamsa's transition to specialist provision

Links between EYFS provision

Hamsa's mother, Yanika, explained that her son's behaviour had really improved since attending the nursery. Previously, she had been to the 'stay and play' sessions at the Children's Centre where staff had raised concerns about his speech and language development. For example, they pointed out that Hamsa did not always respond to his name, and frustration was affecting his behaviour. Yanika did not want Hamsa to be behind in his learning so agreed to a referral to speech and language therapy as well as an audiology assessment. There was a very long wait (approximately 6–7 months) for the appointments to take place, during which time Yanika felt that his behaviour was deteriorating. The Family Support Worker at the Children's Centre helped Yanika secure a free funded place for 2-year-old Hamsa at a private nursery.

Yanika wanted Hamsa to go to the local mainstream school. The Family Support Worker with Yanika arranged a Team Around the Child (TAC) meeting so that everyone involved could talk about ways to support Yanika's plans for Hamsa. The school staff were very helpful, willing to organize support and to visit Hamsa at his nursery in order to see him when he was secure and comfortable. Feeling confident that there would be a local school place for Hamsa, Yanika was then happy to visit a specialist setting with the Family Support Worker. Following this visit and recognizing that there was now a choice to be made about Hamsa's future education, Yanika decided that Hamsa would benefit more from the small groups and the specialist setting rather than the school and so decided that when the time came, Hamsa would take up the place at the specialist setting.

Putting the SEND Code into practice

In each of these narratives it is evident that parents have experienced and valued positive relationships with practitioners. They have found them instrumental in facilitating support for their children, smoothing transitions between provision but also helping them to make informed choices (DfE 2014a: 8, 76). More importantly perhaps, the parents have valued the fact that practitioners have taken a holistic view of their child's needs and listened to their own views. In some cases practitioners have recognized and increased parents' confidence in their own skills and strengths, leading in Lincoln's case to life-changing consequences.

Learning Points

- Positive relationships are characterized by listening carefully to parents and recognizing their strengths and skills
- Transitions are particularly difficult times for parents of children with special educational needs and disabilities; positive relationships across periods of transition are paramount
- Parents rely on practitioners to signpost sources of information and support that in turn help them to make informed choices

Things to think about

- Which of the families of Steven, Josh and Hamsa do you think you would have found most difficult to support in your setting? Why?
- In what ways do you acknowledge and build on parents' existing strengths in your setting?
- In what ways do you plan to improve the relationships across transitions for practitioners and parents?

Early intervention from birth: Gordon, Hugo, Anya and Petra

For some parents the special educational needs and disability journey begins around the birth of their child. This can mean the involvement of a range of professionals, whilst dealing with an overwhelming quantity of information as well as there being many uncertainties about diagnosis and prognosis.

The case studies illustrate:

- the importance of communication between practitioners whilst keeping parents central to any planning and decision-making
- some of the challenges for parents of coordinating appointments, sharing information and dealing with the need to retell their child's story repeatedly
- the covert messages parents receive through the interactions and responses of individual practitioners

The children in the following case studies attended the following early years provision:

- Gordon: childminder
- Hugo: two private day nurseries, a maintained nursery school and an independent special school
- Anya: a private day nursery, a maintained nursery school and an academy
- Petra: a special needs nursery, a maintained nursery school and a local primary school

---

Case study 8:4 Coordinating support for Gordon

Hospital, home and childminder

Gordon's mother, Shirley, felt the family had been really well supported by all those involved in Gordon's care and development. The nurses in the intensive care unit (ICU) were amazing. As her partner had to work, she was often on her own and they really helped her through that difficult time. She felt all the professionals involved had Gordon's best interests at heart. They also listened to her opinions and concerns. Although there was no support from the local health visiting team, the health visitor from ICU was a great support.

Shirley felt though that communication between professionals could be improved. Gordon had around ten monthly appointments which, Shirley felt could be reduced by more phone calls or seeing several specialists together. It was very frustrating, repeating Gordon's history. Keeping track can be difficult leading to uncomfortable feelings of being out of control. Gordon's childminder had been a great practical and emotional support. She had been flexible to accommodate appointments and travel difficulties, but also contributed a professional perspective on Gordon's developmental progress which Shirley communicated to health professionals.

Case study 8:5 Keeping in touch about Hugo

Flexible communication

Hugo's mother, Alison, felt so many aspects of the special educational needs process were out of her control and it was frustrating to be so reliant on others. Mainly, Alison's experiences with the hospital had been good and relationships supportive. Seeing the same consultant each time with excellent communication including email and phone, had been a major factor in helping her feel confident about Hugo's health and care. This partnership with a common purpose also included their GP and was based on mutual respect which acknowledged Alison's and George's specialist understanding of Hugo.

Case study 8:6 Working together for Anya

Collaborative working

Anya has extensive brain damage but with the right support her mother, Ecaterina, believes she has begun and can continue to achieve great things. Ecaterina has found support from Portage workers very helpful as it focused on Anya's abilities rather than on her disabilities and because Ecaterina was involved in planning Anya's 'next steps'.

Ecaterina was very aware of Anya's cognitive abilities and successfully used the 'Your baby can read' programme which meant that Anya could now recognize around 100 words. Ecaterina felt that some health practitioners did not believe the progress Anya was making and whilst they said 'parents know what is best for their children', she believed that they did not mean it. Ecaterina felt that health professionals focused on prevention and maintenance, giving no hope for improvement in the long term.

Ecaterina sees accountability, evidence, motivation and positivity as essential for collaborative working between parents and professionals. She believes it is not as effective if professionals only think about their own specialism, for example, cardiology or neurology, because everyone must see the child as a whole person. She also argues that parents need to communicate clearly what they want for their child so that professionals can give the right support at the right time.

Putting the SEND Code into practice

For parents of children with special educational needs and disabilities the logistics of getting to education, health and care appointments can be extremely difficult – some parents describe it as a 'nightmare'. However, the creation of Education, Health and Care Plans, with the increasing development of joint commissioning, should increase multi-agency collaboration. The SEND Code of Practice is clear that a 'person-centred approach' is required during the Education, Health and Care assessment process (DfE 2014a: 137). In particular, this should bring together relevant professionals and minimize the impact of appointments on family life.

Learning Points

- Effective record-keeping, including family-held records, should reduce occasions when parents are asked to repeat their story and the child's history
- Multi-agency communication, coordination of appointments together with support and contact of parents can improve the quality of help for the child and reduce demands on parents' time and energy

Things to think about

- In your admission procedure, how do you reduce the need for parents to retell their story by reviewing family-held records or information from previous settings?
- In your own record-keeping how do you ensure that the parent's and child's voices are valued and inform your actions?
- In what ways do you seek to understand a parent's perspective of your practice, beyond an annual questionnaire?

Experiences of EYFS provision

For parents whose children have special educational needs or disabilities, experience of EYFS provision continues to be varied. Equally, the links between health and the EYFS are inconsistent and often confusing. The Children and Families Act (2014) and the resultant SEND Code of Practice (DfE 2014a) set out to build local consistency and responsiveness for families and their children. The coordination of support through joint commissioning should increase the capacity for services to work more closely and flexibly together. In the following examples parents explain what a difference this approach and attitude can make to their lives.

The principle of the Unique Child in EYFS can logically be extended to consider the unique family. Practitioners in EYFS play an influential role in welcoming and engaging with children and their families in an enabling environment. This environment is not just physical but also emotional; where appropriate, this also includes a range of practitioners from beyond the setting. From the child and family perspective, variance in quality between settings, practitioners and services is frustrating and increases anxiety about their child's safety.

The case studies illustrate:

- the importance of practitioner attitude and the quality of their relationship with the child and parent
- the value of a common understanding between practitioner and parent who together 'tune into' a child's communication and understand their needs
- practitioners have a key role to play in helping to coordinate support and to work with colleagues to maintain positive relationships with parents

---

Case study 8:7 EYFS experiences for Gordon

Gordon and local authority support

Gordon's mum, Shirley, found the Local Authority Early Years Team very supportive. She was pleased that they had carried out a thorough assessment of Gordon's learning and development needs. This is reviewed regularly, giving suggestions for ways to support Gordon's development, and setting goals so that she and the childminder can help Gordon achieve these.

Case study 8:8 EYFS experience for Hugo

Support from Portage, day nursery, nursery school and the Early Years Inclusion Team

Alison and George reported that early intervention from the Portage Team was very supportive once they began to find their way through the maze of appointments and systems to support Hugo's particular range of needs.

He attended two private day nurseries but these arrangements were unsuccessful. The first would not make physical adjustments to enable Hugo's participation in activities. And, although the second nursery accommodated Hugo's physical needs and were happy for him to attend, Alison quickly felt uncomfortable when she discovered Hugo was being left alone for extended periods in his chair.

At nursery school, Alison and the headteacher agreed that the first priority was to have the right people, with the right training in place to meet Hugo's needs appropriately. The nursery was already an accessible building with standard equipment that included a mobile hoist. The local authority's visual impairment team, occupational health team and physiotherapists visited to contribute to creating a shared plan for his care and educational progress. This would have previously comprised an Individual Education Plan and a Health Care Plan but, following the 2014 SEND Code of Practice, it will be a single Education, Health and Care Plan. The Local Authority Early Years Inclusion Team coordinated the multi-agency support, liaised with practitioners and kept Alison informed. Alison felt that taking Hugo to the nursery school was a positive, stress-free, smooth process.

Like most parents, Alison and George tuned into each of their three children's individual needs and personalities. Specifically, even in those early stages before language developed they understood how and what the children were communicating. Importantly for Alison the practitioners at the nursery quickly understood Hugo too and ensured consistency of love and care through the Key Person approach. They showed respect for him by maintaining appropriate routines while administering medication and when feeding and changing him.

Alison emphasized that acknowledging Hugo as a person and an important member of his family really made a difference. Alison sees her role, as well as being a mum, as Hugo's voice, fighting for him as she would for other members of her family. She reflected that, as a parent of a child with complex needs, it is important to present an attitude that communicates assertiveness but also reliability and consistency.

When Hugo progressed to a local independent special school for children with profound, multiple learning and complex medical needs, he continued to return to the nursery school for the after-school club and the holiday play scheme. Hugo enjoys his special school, and his parents, Alison and George, are very happy with the provision and relationships with practitioners.

Case study 8:9 EYFS experience for Anya

Attending day nursery, nursery school and academy

During the time Anya attended the day nursery Ecaterina felt near to tears in review meetings because there were always reasons that experiences suggested by Portage had not been implemented. According to practitioners, they found it 'just too difficult to support Anya'. Ecaterina commented that the manager was a caring person who didn't realize the covert message she was giving about the day nursery's attitudes to children with special needs.

However at nursery school, the attitudes were very different, with a much greater focus on Anya's progress and everyone contributing to any problem-solving. The nursery included Anya in all activities so that she developed positive relationships with children and adults. She can now cope with children coming close to her, has two particularly close relationships and has been to friends' birthday parties. After this success, leaving the nursery to move on to school was a huge step in her mother's view and she cried about losing the genuine feeling of working together as a team for Anya.

Moving on to a reception class in school meant new relationships not only for Anya but also for Ecaterina, her mother. But after her first visit she felt positive and since first impressions were good, when she received a letter from the school offering Anya a place, Ecaterina and her husband felt the school was welcoming Anya 'with open arms'. This was further reinforced when the class teacher visited their home and the nursery school, and appeared to be very at ease with Anya.

In her discussion with the Chief Executive of the Academy Trust about the school Anya was to attend, Ecaterina understood more clearly the differences between the very formal schools she was familiar with in her own country, Romania, and the play-based approach to learning in her English primary school. Discussions also included how all adults would be enabled to work with Anya. It was agreed that rather than her being assigned one person for the 20 hours of funded support through the statement of special educational needs, the school would instead ensure that Anya was given generous support by all the adults in the reception class.

Case study 8:10 EYFS experience for Petra

Attending nursery school

Rosalind, Petra's mother, was delighted with the progress Petra had made at the nursery school, especially in reading and conversation skills, exceeding all expectations! She had an amazing Key Person who was confident and relaxed with Petra. Although Petra would often refuse to do things at home, at nursery she tried new things and engaged with other children. She is developing confidence, independence, and learning from the appropriate behaviour of her peers too.

The transition from special needs nursery to mainstream nursery was very successful. Rosalind felt 'led' by friendly and experienced professionals in both settings. They worked well together without making her feel left out. The special needs nursery staff, who knew Petra so well, ensured that all necessary information was passed to the mainstream nursery team who were eager to learn about her. The mainstream practitioners took all the information on board easily and did not appear scared or hesitant about Petra's future attendance, this was very different from what Rosalind had experienced when she had approached other settings.

Putting the SEND Code into practice

These case studies indicate a wide variation of practice in welcoming and including children with special educational needs and their families. This variation contributes to parents' believing that they have to fight for appropriate support and provision for their child. The EYFS is the start of this educational journey for children from birth to 5 years and consequently it is usually early years practitioners who set the tone and expectations for parents (DfE 2014a: 70) of children with special educational needs. When practitioners are able to implement the EYFS principle of the Unique Child, inclusive, responsive practice follows.

As no doubt you will have concluded, the disconnect between the setting described as 'happy to make physical adjustments' to their provision but then finding themselves unable to include Hugo in daily activities was shocking. The contrast with his next setting where practitioners demonstrated care, empathy and an understanding of him as an individual is stark. One is left with anxiety about the quality of care for all other children attending the first setting Hugo attended. However, this startling example also provides a vignette of effective practice for children with special educational needs illustrating that what is effective practice in relation to children with special needs is consistent with high quality experiences for all children. Problem-solving, mediation and negotiation are core skills for all practitioners, especially SENCOs.

Learning Points

- EYFS provision provides a template for families about what to expect from the education sector for their children with special needs and themselves
- There should be consistency between what we say, do and believe about implementing the principles of the EYFS since these influence our engagement with all families
- Individual attitudes are central to inclusive approaches and to the success of high quality EYFS provision

---

Things to think about

- In what ways do you demonstrate the EYFS principles during your admission process? Does this extend to areas of disagreement with parents, for example, some parents may have strongly-held beliefs with which you disagree?
- Select five words to describe your current attitude to working with children with special educational needs. Why have you selected these – are they consistent with the stated 'mission' of the setting?
- How many inconsistencies can you identify between SEN policy and practice in your setting between:

  ○ individuals
  ○ room teams
  ○ SENCO and the rest of the leadership team

Multi-agency assessment leading to Education, Health and Care Plans

A common trigger for repeated reviews of the special educational needs assessment process has been dissatisfaction voiced by parents. Indeed, Mary Warnock herself suggested that as a process it was no longer fit for purpose (Warnock and Norwich 2010: 10).

The following case studies support this view and give insights into personal experiences. In particular, they illustrate:

- that parents can experience the process as difficult, adversarial and confusing but having a knowledgeable professional as a 'guide' makes this more manageable
- how tensions about the availability of places and numbers of applications, with local authorities as both providers and arbiters of the process, can often leave parents feeling in competition, but also overwhelmed and frustrated
- the fact that practical considerations for all children in the family are seldom taken into account, for example, differences in the picking-up and dropping-off times of different settings
- how at annual reviews, because of local authority funding restrictions there can be additional uncertainty about the continuity of provision for a child in a particular setting

---

Case study 8:11 Hugo's journey to special school

Independent special school

Alison, Hugo's mother, remembers the assessment process as long and stressful. Knowing there were more children than special school places, meant visiting provision, finding the one you wanted, then competing with other families. Ideally, his parents would have liked Hugo to continue at the nursery school for another year but they thought that delaying special school application would reduce the chances of his securing a place. Also with independently run special schools, like Hugo's, there was always a risk the local authority would not continue to fund the placement.

Repeating their story when there were changes in his provision was a frustration for Alison and George. It was very emotional and meant revisiting unsatisfactory, unsettling or distressful times and events. In addition, to access support, Alison felt they needed to give the worst possible view of Hugo's abilities to make sure that he received his entitlement. As parents this was very difficult and seemed to deny the progress Hugo had made.

Alison described making visits to specialist provision as a shock. As she watched the older children, it was as if she was confronted by a vision of Hugo's possible future. On her second visit she felt more able to decide whether or not the school could meet Hugo's current needs.

The school Family Liaison Worker was welcoming and talked about what the school could offer Hugo and his family, which really helped.

Alison recalled that it felt as though she was on 'their side' from the beginning. The curriculum was perfect for Hugo since it was more sensory than that in the local authority special school. Also he would be able to attend there until he was 18 years old, provided the annual review process confirmed it continued to be the most appropriate provision.

Case study 8:12 Anya's application for mainstream school

The Early Support Coordinator as a guide through the system

Having the Early Support Coordinator as a guide gave Ecaterina, Anya's mother, confidence and helped her make sense of the processes. Ecaterina felt that 'as a parent you have lots of questions but it can be hard to make sense of the answers, and the implications for your own child'. Ecaterina had strong views about which school she felt would be most appropriate for Anya. She was especially concerned that Anya's cognitive abilities would be recognized and supported. Not all the professionals involved during Anya's multi-agency assessment agreed with this view.

The Early Support Coordinator helped Ecaterina to apply for a local academy. In Ecaterina's contribution to the statutory assessment (since the 2014 SEND Code of Practice this is known as the Education, Health and Care Plan), she made a detailed case, including financial and educational arguments addressing all the likely issues the local authority might raise to prevent Anya attending mainstream provision. Ecaterina understood she needed to advocate and be prepared to fight. Articulating her aspirations and reviewing the evidence from the multi-agency assessments with the Early Support Coordinator helped Ecaterina rehearse her arguments, and build a strong and convincing case.

Case study 8:13 Finding a school for Petra

Fighting the system

Rosalind, Petra's mother, explains, 'To be honest being a mum in the special needs world is exhausting and if you don't know who to ask, you will not get what you need for your child.' Rosalind worked with the Children with Disability Team before Petra was born so she knew when she realized that Petra's development was atypical who should be involved, what to ask for and when to make certain demands. Petra was in a very good special needs nursery which supported the transition to an excellent mainstream nursery. Rosalind felt it was important not to feel overwhelmed or to think that all professionals are right, but to ask challenging questions to ensure that the final plan for Petra would be correct. She reported that the educational psychologist wrote a completely inaccurate report – one apparently written by someone with no knowledge of Petra and which also disregarded previous reports. Rosalind was given no advice about choosing schools so spent months making visits independently and without any support. Often as a parent, Rosalind reported feeling that she was overreacting or asking for too much. Luckily she explained, she knew how to complain and have things put right. She asserted that she thought it important that other parents were 'empowered to do that too'.

Putting the SEND Code into practice

It can be difficult to understand how our provision feels to those coming to it from 'outside'. Further, the systems we use have developed over time, and if not reviewed at regular intervals can grow to include lengthy and unnecessary form filling. Engaging parents and new practitioners in this review process can be a useful way to harness the value of an 'outside' perspective.

Supporting parents whose children have emerging or recognized special educational needs requires practitioners, especially SENCOs who are confident and knowledgeable about local processes. Contributing to and keeping informed about the Local Authority local offer but also being up to date on schools' annual SEN Information Report is therefore essential (DfE 2014a: 48, 95).

Learning Points

- Understanding the local offer, including processes, timescales and availability of specialist places enables informed conversations with parents and leads to realistic expectations
- Having to constantly repeat their story is not just frustrating but an emotional and often disheartening experience for parents
- Tuning into the parents' emotional as well as factual communication can reduce tensions and support informed decision-making
- Reflecting with parents after a transition, implementing an EHCP or a multi-agency meeting can inform future improvement of the parent–child experience

---

Things to think about

- Attending and contributing appropriately to a multi-agency meeting is a skilful and valuable professional development. What discussions have you had in supervision to identify ways to develop your practice in this area?
- What links do you have with local specialist provision, including making visits to the setting, joint activities or contact between practitioners?
- In what ways do your setting's systems, processes and provision complement the local offer?

Conclusion: advice to other parents

The conclusion to this chapter is communicated by some of the parents who given their own experiences. They offer their personal advice to other parents who may find themselves in a similar situation.

Jane

- When you first realize your child has special needs you feel your world has gone but it hasn't, you need to get to know your child really well, to understand him as a person, the things he likes, needs and is good at. This lets you help others to get to know him, understand him and help him.
- The manager/SENCO has been an emotional support too. Sometimes it is important to be able to cry with the people who are helping you.
- The local Children's Centre was a good place to go because they listened and helped with practical things like filling in forms for Disability Living Allowance and they made a referral for a place at nursery.

Yanika

- The staff at nursery were especially supportive, caring and patient. Parents and practitioners need to see that every child has different needs and to get to know them well to understand the best help for them and their family at a particular time.

Rosalind

- Don't keep quiet if you are worried about anything; professionals do not know your child as well as you do. Professionals do have experience, so listen and learn from them, but do not hesitate to disagree or get a second opinion if you do not feel that they are doing the best for your child.
- We have encountered amazing people who have provided Petra with wonderful support and really made a difference. However, we have also encountered those, who for a variety of reasons, do not have the time or inclination to do their best for her.

Ecaterina

- Don't despair, you need to keep listening to the positive messages from those around you. Support groups are good for getting information and can offer emotional support. But no support group has the power to give the total peace and strength that God can give.
- Ecaterina then suggests that the most powerful and motivating tool a non-believer could have is love. In particular, love for their child, which Ecaterina relates directly to the passage in the Bible which states 'and now these three remain faith, hope and love. But the greatest of these is love' (1 Corinthians 13: 13).
- She says: 'In selecting a school placement as much as you want your child not to feel different, a special school may not be the right place in the long term. Specialist provision is likely to be comfortable but may lack the challenge and high expectations to develop a child's independence to live in the real world, with a positive sense of themselves. In your aspirations for your child make the most of their ability not disability.'

Improving and developing practice

- From your personal and professional knowledge what challenges have parents experienced as they explored appropriate provision for their child with special educational needs? What more could you, your setting and practitioners have done to support them further?

- In what ways have you increased your knowledge and under-standing of local special educational needs provision in your area over the past six months?
- How could you increase your confidence in building positive rela-tionships with all parents?

Key Points

- Although practitioners may go through the process of multi-agency assessment several times with different children, parents will usually only do it once. Listening carefully to parent's views helps us to recognize the 'emotional roller coaster' they are often experiencing. This understanding helps us to reflect on the most effective way to support their decision-making.
- Being a parent is frequently challenging as well as wonderful. Finding yourself trying to make sense of a 'special educational needs' process can be one of those challenges. Practitioners, especially SENCOs, play an important role in building parents' confidence as advocates for their child.
- Daily practice in a setting can easily become rooted in a 'we've always done it this way' approach as well as resistance to change. Striving to understand a parent's or child's perspective can enable us to make adjustments that accommodate their needs but also revitalize our practice.

9   The child's perspective

Chapter themes

- The importance of building, with their parents, a common understanding of each child

- Collating information from different aspects of a child's life to deepen our understanding of their current experiences

- Using our understanding of each child's views to reflect on and improve our practice with all children

The historical perspective outlined at the beginning of this book illustrated a tremendous lack of opportunity for parents, let alone children, to have their say about the nature of provision or support available to them. As attitudes to equalities and disabilities have progressed, it is clear that the views of those needing the support must be heard for an increasingly effective system to evolve.

The importance of listening to children is set out in the UN Convention on the Rights of the Child signed by the UK in 1991. Article 12:1 states,

> States Parties shall assure to the child who is capable of forming his or her own views the right to express those views freely in all matters affecting the child, the views of the child being given due weight in accordance with the age and maturity of the child.
>
> (UNICEF 1990)

The Children and Families Act (2014) states that local authorities, 'must have regard to:

- the views, wishes and feelings of the child or young person, and the child's parents
- the importance of the child or young person and the child's parents, participating as fully as possible in decisions, and being provided with the information and support necessary to enable participation in those decisions

(HMSO 2014: 8)

Being able to articulate our views is a complex skill that develops throughout our life span. It is strongly influenced by whether or not we are 'heard' and have an impact on the events and people in our lives. Children learn a lot about this process in the EYFS period. The power dynamic will inevitably be weighted towards the adult, but the essential point is whether or not the adult uses this power to enable or disable the child's ability to contribute and to be heard.

The principle of the Unique Child is at the heart of the EYFS framework. Accommodating the child's voice increases our ability to support their learning and development. Given that for most children in the EYFS, verbal and writing skills are emerging, other means of communication must be explored. This approach was explored in the National Children's Bureau (NCB) initiative the Young Children's Voices Network project which ran from 2006 to 2011. The NCB worked with local authorities to identify and support effective practice, particularly in the early years. Listening effectively to children's views and ensuring that they were used to inform policy was identified as leading to positive outcomes for children, parents, practitioners and local authorities (Clark 2011: 1). The Young Children's Voices Network defined 'listening' as:

> an active process of receiving (hearing and observing), interpreting and responding to communication – it includes all the senses and emotions and is not limited to the spoken word.

This inclusive approach is an integral element of effective early years pedagogy and an essential part of tuning into children as individuals in the context of their families and communities.

As early years practitioners we are aware that from birth babies are communicating, they 'tell' us if they are comfortable or uncomfortable. They also let us know how they prefer to be held and how to give them comfort. This is true of all children (whether they have special educational needs or not).

Parents are sensitive and motivated to understand their baby's communication whether in response to a wriggle or a piercing cry. Building on this we observe and tune in to babies, using this starting point to deepen our ability to listen to all children. This requires us to be open in our interactions and prepared to take the things the children are communicating to us seriously. Consequently, if as professionals we do this, there is an inherent expectation that we will act on what has been said. It is this experience of being 'listened to' and having their views acted upon which is so important in empowering children to believe they have a voice, especially when this is not a verbal one.

Key Person and common purpose

A sense of common purpose in early years provision should be evident in the practice of all practitioners, providing a support for them as well as the children. In previous chapters we have explored the perspectives of leaders and SENCOs yet the Key Person also plays a crucial role in relating to children and their families.

In Chapters 7 and 8 we met Hugo and Anya and considered the support they and their families received from their maintained nursery school. We also met Darren in Chapter 5 and now we are introduced to Daniel and Peter. Together with their parents Daniel and Peter's Key Persons have learned about their individual personality and forms of communication. The case studies are taken from the perspectives of these Key Persons and illustrate:

- the importance of a Key Person getting to know each child as an individual personality and a competent learner
- how continuity of the expressed purpose of the setting to 'meet the needs of children and families in the local community' translates into practice
- examples of collaborative working between practitioners

The case studies illustrate a variety of ways that practitioners skilfully gain insights into a child's perspective. They have used observation, conversations with parents and techniques adapted to the child's individual needs to enable their voices to be heard and their views to be acted upon. In Case study 8:1, Maureen, a very experienced teaching assistant, working in a maintained nursery school is responsible for Peter, a 4-year-old, recently diagnosed with Autistic Spectrum Disorder (ASD). In discussion, Maureen explained that often when a practitioner learns a new child is coming to the nursery the initial information about their medical conditions, special educational needs and disabilities can seem challenging and may create uncertainty about how well one can cope as a Key Person to a particular child. Taking responsibility for that child can also feel overwhelming at times, but, according to Maureen, 'with knowledge, information and positive relationships with parents and carers, these feelings soon subside'. And, of course, she added: 'Once you know the child as an individual, the fear reduces because you start to think about them as a person and not a condition or disability.'

Tuning into the child

Every child is different, but the first step is to make a connection that is both positive and two-way. Maureen describes how she often uses singing and gentle sounds to engage the child. In looking for a response it is important to observe the child's whole body identifying any small movements or changes. As responses are noted, talking with parents helps to work out the meaning of different sounds and movements. Gradually, together a picture is built up of how this particular child is communicating and how to recognize and interpret the sounds they make. And, whilst communicating without language is something we all do, it is easy to forget how difficult it can be to make one's needs known if one has little or no language to clarify one's meaning. Maureen believes it is important to continually find ways to be responsive and open to children's whole body communication, tuning into each child in the moment, understanding their intention, motivation and communication. 'It is,' she says, 'about understanding how would you like to be treated and striving to do that for others.'

This case study illustrates:

- responsiveness to Peter's emotions
- 'moment-to-moment' planning based on secure understanding of Peter and his approaches to learning
- recognizing the importance of fun in the learning process

Case study 9:1 Peter and his Key Person, Maureen

Working with an individual child – skills, strategies and approaches

The short activity session consisted of play with two inset puzzles and a storybook with sound effects. Peter was particularly sensitive to loud noises so the storybook gave him an opportunity to have fun and enjoy different sounds whilst being in control of the noises made. From her knowledge of Peter, Maureen had constructed the session to include simple and familiar routines, as well as things that he would enjoy. She created a context in which Peter quickly relaxed.

Peter demonstrated several strong patterns in his responses. However, Maureen's subtle interventions offered compromise and helped him to accept some of the adult agenda rather than just his own. For example, with the inset puzzles Maureen respected his approach but made small changes such as maintaining the order in which pieces were added. Familiar signs such as 'finish', 'more' and 'thumbs up' and repeated phrases like 'Are you ready?', 'Where is the . . .?', 'first', 'next one' and 'thank you, Peter' were repeated and helped to structure the activity for Peter.

By integrating Makaton, a sign and symbol communication system, with language and varying her tone and intonation Maureen's communication of meaning was clearer for Peter. Her intonation and facial expressions throughout signalled her support but also real pleasure at his success; he then mirrored this by smiling and giggling back. Maureen gave Peter control of the order of activities by offering choice between two puzzles.

A further focus of the activity was to provide appropriate vocabulary and repetitive phrases to support Peter's actions and thinking. Importantly, Maureen also sensitively listened to Peter's vocalizations, interpreting sounds as well as meaning based on her previous experience of being with him.

Knowing the ending was likely to cause particular anxiety, Maureen helped Peter to cope with this. For the whole 15-minute session Peter was engaged and increasingly relaxed. This culminated in sharing the sound book when there was real chuckling and fun shared by Maureen and Peter.

Putting the SEND Code into practice

This detailed example demonstrates that seemingly elusive 'high quality' practice may be quite simply about following and leading the child in a communicative dance – and, far from being unobtainable, it is achievable as long as we are guided by the child's needs. In Appendix 5 there is an example of a play plan supporting Peter's progress. After exploring recent observations, Maureen had agreed with parents and colleagues the priorities for Peter's 'next steps' and used these to plan the content of the next activity session. However, because of her in-depth knowledge of Peter she was also able to be flexible and responsive to him during the session. As the sample play plan shows, Peter exceeded her expectations by being able to maintain engagement for an additional five minutes and by his obvious enjoyment of the sound book. In this session she was able to use 'moment-by-moment' planning as she supported him to progress further including introducing the repeated phrase 'Where is the . . .?' to increase her involvement in his completion of the jigsaw puzzles.

Things to think about

- Which child in your setting do feel you know best? How have you talked with parents about your interpretations of their emotions which are communicated through facial expressions, changes in body language signing or verbal responses?
- In which activities do you notice the combination of fun and learning happening most for children? How are these opportunities planned for?
- In what ways is the child's perspective represented in your planning process?

Daniel

Case study 9:2 introduces Daniel and illustrates:

- the value of home visits
- the importance of detailed observation and understanding of Daniel's communication
- how Daniel is given the opportunity to communicate his views about his learning

Case study 9:2 Daniel and his Key Person, Maria

Special school EYFS provision for children with Autistic Spectrum Disorder (ASD)

Prior to Daniel starting school, Maria, his Key Person, planned a home visit. With his parents' permission, she recorded information gathered on an 'All About Me' form. This included questions about Daniel's communication, likes and dislikes, strengths, diet, as well as any known triggers for certain behaviours, his self-care skills and his broader physical skills. Maria discovered that Daniel liked physical activities such as jumping and climbing and that he also liked drawing, colouring, puzzles and playing on the computer. He communicated using gestures and some single words. He was able to approach adults for reassurance and happily played independently. He followed directions but needed time to process information. This understanding of Daniel helped make preparation for his transition into school more responsive to his needs.

Now in school, Daniel prefers to play alone but will sometimes play alongside others, and accept other children joining his play. He enjoys climbing and balancing and jumping on the trampoline, accepting an adult will hold his hands to help him jump higher. He will happily give eye contact and smiles. He concentrates best in self-chosen art and craft activities. He will cry if he thinks he has made a mistake in his drawing but with reassurance will settle and continue. Daniel likes to build towers and knock them down. He likes to play in the sand using different tools to fill containers. Daniel particularly likes to play the keyboard.

Maria devised a 'Child's Views' form using photos and symbols, enabling Daniel to communicate what he enjoys, whom he likes to be with (adults and children) and what he recognizes as his strengths. He also communicated that he wanted to 'be better at' building towers with a friend.

Putting the SEND Code into practice

By making the home visit Maria was able to meet Daniel in his most familiar environment. Her observations gave a sound basis for realistic expectations of how he would adjust to school. The process of gathering children's views needs to allow for a range of communication methods but most importantly the adults have to be open and attentive. It is always a danger that we make assumptions about a child's view from our knowledge of them rather than truly 'listening' to their communication.

Learning Points

- Avoiding making assumptions about a child's views means adults need to have an open attitude to 'listening' to the child's communication, rather than having preconceived ideas
- Children who are able to express their views verbally also benefit from the opportunity to use photos, signs and symbols to communicate
- Creating an environment where children feel their views are valued takes time and constant monitoring to ensure that adult responses give a consistent message, especially if they 'disagree' with the child's view

Things to think about

- In what ways do you currently seek the views of the children in your setting?
- Describe the context and process that are most effective for this. Why do they work so well?
- What happens if there is any discrepancy between the views of practitioners, parents and children about the child's strengths, difficulties, friends or ways of learning?

Darren

We learnt about Darren's progress in Chapter 5 but here specific extracts highlight how the practitioners in the day nursery listened to his communication. When Darren was around 20 months old the day nursery practitioners had concerns that his physical development was not progressing as expected.

This case study illustrates:

- the importance of observation underpinned by a desire to understand Darren's communication
- how Darren's views had been heard
- the positive impact on Darren's learning of being 'listened' to

Case study 9:3 Darren and his Key Person, Olivia

Looking to understand

Olivia, a practitioner, used focused observations and team discussions to identify ways of encouraging Darren to reach, stretch, crawl and shuffle. She used the activities he enjoyed most, with treasure baskets a particular success. Olivia selected objects that really attracted his attention. At first, the treasure basket was placed near but just out of Darren's reach yet he happily stretched to catch hold of the objects. Gradually, Olivia moved the basket a little further away and placed some of the objects on the mat around Darren. He increasingly enjoyed reaching and crawling to get his favourite objects.

Detailed observation showed that Darren liked banging things together. Olivia quickly recognized it was not the movement itself but the sound that engaged him, and his favourite noise was the 'clang' of two metal bowls when he banged them together. Rainmakers, bells, bubble wrap and switches extended his interest in sound making. Practitioners added voiced sounds which he increasingly mimicked before developing his own. Olivia understood Darren's responses as if he had been having a conversation with her about his interests and fascinations.

Putting the SEND Code into practice

Olivia used a combination of detailed observation and discussion with others to develop her understanding of Darren. Recognizing the responses that indicated his enjoyment and engagement in an activity enabled her to focus on the things, such as sounds, that fascinated him. The journey, from helping him stretch and move to increasing his verbalization, was supported and accelerated by Olivia's close observation and analysis of what she had seen him do. This case study demonstrates the difference between simply observing the activity as an isolated event and focusing on its meaning for the child — the child's perspective.

Learning Points

- Olivia's attitude was open to Darren's communication, she was looking to understand his behaviour
- Darren's communication was valued and acted upon to enhance his learning
- Understanding the child's perspective can help us support their learning more effectively

---

Things to think about

- When do you take time to discuss the detail of observations with parents and colleagues to improve everybody's understanding of a particular child?
- In the past three weeks, how have you demonstrated your understanding of a child's views? How have you acted on them?
- What action have you taken to listen more effectively to the children you find hardest to engage with?

Hugo

Hugo, who also featured in Chapter 8, attended nursery school before moving to a local independent special school. Hugo has complex special educational needs, including physical, sensory and cognitive impairments. His mother, Alison, felt that the practitioners at the nursery school, especially Michelle, his Key Person, quickly demonstrated their principle of 'recognizing each child as an individual' particularly during the 'settling-in' period.

This case study illustrates:

- how parents and practitioners worked together successfully to understand Hugo's communication
- how the Key Person was able to recognize and predict Hugo's needs accurately and sensitively
- how 'being listened to' encourages children to communicate more

Case study 9:4 Hugo and his Key Person, Michelle

Learning from parents

In partnership with Alison, practitioners ensured that they were seeing and understanding Hugo's signals, such as closing his eyes when he was not interested in something, or making particular noises to communicate his feelings and needs. Alison felt the practitioners were very quick to pick up on his signals because of their willingness to start a positive relationship with him. Alison described Hugo's relationship with Michelle as 'very loving, caring and respectful'. Michelle, she feels, is really in tune with him, continually making sure he is happy and comfortable. She is skilled in recognizing when he wants time out of his chair with other children, but also knows when he has had enough, wants another activity or needs time to rest.

Hugo is clearly happy when he goes to the setting, showing he is at ease with the adults who care for him through the way he demonstrates his pleasure when he recognizes their voices. To accurately 'hear' Hugo's voice, all the adults have worked closely together to recognize and interpret his signals. These signals can be very subtle, including changes in the noises he is making, blinking his eyes and a range of body movements. By this 'listening', the adults are also encouraging him to communicate more, affecting his immediate experience, making choices and having some control over his environment and those who care for him.

Putting the SEND Code into practice

Everyone communicates in a range of ways though we often rely on verbal communication perhaps because it seems easier. However, tuning into the more subtle changes in body language, facial expression and demeanour with the desire to understand allows a much richer channel of communication. Where parents and practitioners work together, helping each other to recognize and interpret a child's communication, the sense of being listened to is much more profound for the child. For Hugo, being listened to effectively enabled him to have more control over his immediate environment and motivated him to increase his communication.

Learning Points

- Michelle is motivated to try to see the world from Hugo's perspective (as she does with the other children in her Key Person group)
- The quality of the relationship between Michelle and Hugo complements the relationship with his parents
- As parents and practitioners are working so closely, Hugo experiences continuity and coherence in his relationships contributing to his feelings of being valued and listened to

Things to think about

- What would be the challenges and delights of including Hugo in your setting?
- In what ways do you support your colleagues to recognize children's nonverbal communication, using it positively to understand the child's views?
- In what ways could you develop how you communicate with parents about their child's views?

Anya

Anya, whom we first read about in Chapter 8, has complex special educational needs including physical, sensory and cognitive impairments. Socially, her mother, Ecaterina, feels there have been major improvements for Anya while at nursery. The relationships with practitioners have been very positive especially with her Key Person, Yvonne.

This case study illustrates:

- the importance of listening to children's views in relation to their emotions
- why we should have realistic expectations of the ebb and flow of energy and mood for individuals
- the significance of encouraging children's friendships for all children but especially those with special educational needs

Case study 9:5 Anya and her Key Person, Yvonne

Anya in nursery school

Ecaterina felt that the practitioners at the nursery school were keen to listen to and understand Anya's communication. They really seemed able to see Anya as an individual person who was able to make choices, and have preferences about who she interacted with, as well as likes and dislikes in food, clothes, etc. Most importantly they understood that, like all of us, Anya could have good days and not so good days. Yvonne recognized that Anya preferred to watch an activity first before taking part. She particularly liked to engage in activities that adults had introduced and which were familiar.

Anya learnt to enjoy the company of other children because the practitioners, especially Yvonne, helped the relationships to develop. They focused on appropriate activities that Anya preferred and as other children joined in, they were helped to interpret Anya's communication as a natural part of their play. Anya developed some special friendships with the children typically checking on arrival to see if they had already arrived.

Anya made her feelings known using a range of verbal sounds to communicate which became louder if she felt upset or cross. She also used facial expressions, signing and the computer to communicate. Now she particularly finds music soothing and likes being cuddled by her favourite people.

Putting the SEND Code into practice

Seeing children as individuals and recognizing differences as well as similarities are a major part of their growing awareness of each other during their time in EYFS. The attitudes demonstrated by practitioners are crucial in enabling children to feel at ease with each other, make choices about friendships, and begin to understand each other's displays of emotions. Yvonne's understanding of Anya as well as of the other children helped her to recognize the relationships that were meaningful and important to them.

Learning Points

- It is unrealistic to expect children (or adults) to be happy and relaxed all the time. EYFS is a time when children are increasingly aware of each other, forming temporary alliances as well as deep, long-lasting friendships. Children often display the full range of emotions as they learn about themselves and ways to deal with their feelings
- An important role for the Key Person is to ensure their engagement in the developing social world of the setting. This is especially true when the child has special educational needs or disabilities
- Understanding how a child communicates specific emotions helps us learn about what calms, excites, saddens and cheers them. As adults reflect this understanding, they contribute to a child's ability to self-regulate

Things to think about

- What is your typical response to a child's display of the following emotional states and what learning does this response lead to for you and the child?

  - angry
  - sad
  - frightened
  - happy
  - worried

- In what ways are children supported to positively understand each other's emotions?
- What realistic messages do practitioners give in your setting about the importance of making friends, the qualities of a good friend and ways to sustain friendships when the going gets tough?

The previous case studies show how practitioners worked closely with parents to understand and engage with the children in their Key Person group. However, it is important to accept that this is not always easy or something which 'just happens'. For the Key Person it takes effort, skill and a positive attitude to make the relationships work so well. Beginning this process with a child with special educational needs or disabilities may seem daunting at first.

As detailed in the National Children's Bureau, Young Children's Voices Network leaflet, *Listening as a Way of Life* (Clark 2011), we listen to children:

- because it acknowledges their right to be listened to and for their views and experiences to be taken seriously
- because of the difference listening can make to our understanding of children's priorities, interests and concerns
- because of the difference it can make to our understanding of how children feel about themselves
- because listening is a vital part of establishing respectful relationships with the children we work with and is central to the learning process

Further information and case studies related to the Young Children's Voices Network are available via the internet, and specific examples worth exploring include Northamptonshire (available on www.Northampton.gov.uk), the Pre-school Learning Alliance (available from www.pre-school.org.uk), and the London Borough of Ealing.

Since the 2006 Children's Act there have been several initiatives to increase awareness of ascertaining and acting on the views of children and young people. This includes children with disabilities through innovations such as Voice, Inclusion, Participation, Empowerment and Research (VIPER), Making Ourselves Heard (MOH), and Equality, Participation, Influence and Change (EPIC). Organizations such as the Council for Disabled Children, the Centre for Studies on Inclusive Education (CSIE), and Disability Rights UK continue to promote the development of services for those with disabilities designed and informed by those with disabilities.

Improving and developing practice

- What would help you to feel more confident about being the Key Person for a child with complex needs?
- In what ways do you offer colleagues genuine collaboration in tuning into individual children's communication and needs?
- Working with which child in your Key Group has improved your practice most in the past six months?

Key Points

- Confidence in working with children with special educational needs comes from experience and learning from, as well as with, parents and colleagues
- Tuning into each Unique Child by building a detailed understanding of their verbal and non-verbal communication underpins effective high quality interaction and positive relationships
- Appreciating other's perspectives adds to our own understanding and encourages creative problem-solving as we work together to improve our practice with all children

10 Looking to the future

Chapter themes

- Inclusive practice in EYFS
- Individual influence on practice in EYFS
- A way forward

Inclusive practice in EYFS

As we have seen in previous chapters, in settings where there is high quality practice, practitioners reflect and challenge their practice, keeping fresh their common purpose of meeting individual children's needs. There are many aspects to practice which require improvement and maintenance and at times it seems incredible that it can all come together in expert performance. The structures and systems outlined in the EYFS offer a tried and tested framework to support continuously improving practice. The explicit focus on the Unique Child, with skilled professionals recognizing developmentally significant progress, in partnership with parents, is a secure basis. The challenge is to know what high quality 'looks' and 'feels' like on any particular day. The intention of this book has been to explore some of that 'high quality' in order to support individual reflection and personal challenge.

The Children and Families Act (2014), and the SEND Code of Practice (DfE 2014a) though reinforcing the principles of the EYFS will inevitably lead to changes in early years practice. However, this may not be radical enough to change some of the significant barriers experienced by some parents and their children with special needs – whether these are the tensions of timescales, availability of specialist places, or funding issues. The publication of the 'local offer' at authority and school level will, however, support parents to make more informed decisions, and could also be a significant driver for change, as parents and young people become more involved in the review of local provision.

Most obviously, the opportunity to reflect on the role of the SENCO in the EYFS presents itself. Explicitly, implementing the setting approach to SEN support involving the graduated response of the 'assess, plan, do, review' cycle and, linking with services beyond the setting and engaging with the local offer. Implicitly, the role will involve the SENCO in becoming a leader of practice in meeting the needs of the Unique Child through early intervention, whilst maintaining an overview of rates and patterns of progress to facilitate early identification of special educational needs. Inevitably this will highlight the disparity between the role of the SENCO in an EYFS setting compared with that of SENCOs in the primary and secondary settings, particularly since introduction of the requirement for SENCOs in those phases to complete the National Award for SENCO qualification introduced in 2008. This elevated SENCOs to become members of the leadership team and acknowledged the need for non-contact time to fulfil the role effectively (Hallett and Hallet 2010: 18). Sadly, the opportunity to level the playing field between EYFS, primary and secondary SENCOs has not been realized through this latest SEND Code of Practice. However, it is to be hoped that the increasing priority given to early intervention and cross-party interest in childcare and special needs issues may yet see targeted funding for training and greater recognition of this important role.

Individual influences on practice in EYFS

As we have seen in our examination of SEN in early years, the crucial ingredient which affects the experience of children and families is not the documentation or legislation but the nature of relationships encountered by parents and children. The Children and Families Act (2014) has tried to capture this in the phrase 'using their best endeavours' but the words are cheap if an inclusive attitude is not a daily reality for families. It is only through an inclusive ethos that each practitioner can be supported to develop an inclusive attitude. Case studies have been used to highlight the use of supervision and collaborative working to enhance understanding of a common purpose and professional development. Strong professional relationships with colleagues enabling challenge, reflection and growing confidence cannot be underestimated but need conscious nurturing. Leadership, characterized by setting high expectations, using supervision and coaching to achieve the common purpose is most likely to result in continuous improvement (Cook 2013: 43). Supervision is a crucial link between theory and practice, for example conscious decisions need to be made about supporting independence, autonomy and social connection rather than allowing children to become dependent on adults and isolated from social engagement with others in a setting. Training and supervision play a key role in developing an understanding of this perspective and the possible impact of support.

In Case study 10:1 the strong leadership of the headteacher has embedded a culture of an inclusive community in a nursery school. Through coaching, mentoring and supervision all practitioners understand this common purpose of meeting each child's individual needs and demonstrate it in their everyday interactions.

Case study 10:1 Creating an inclusive community

Every interaction is important

Eleanor, an experienced teaching assistant, communicates the nursery school's tenet that every child is part of the community through conversations with children about their own and other's needs enabling them to find out about and understand each other. For example, answering children's questions honestly when asked about a child using a wheelchair.

> CHILD: Why does Ella needed a wheelchair?
> ELEANOR: Ella's legs don't work.
> CHILD: Will they ever work?
> ELEANOR: Y'know, I don't know the answer to that, one day they might, but maybe they never will.

Eleanor sees these incidental conversations as opportunities to provide appropriate vocabulary but also factual understanding for children. The underlying message for the children is that such conversations are valued and an important part of their learning.

A longer-term gain that Eleanor has noted is that the children can teach their parents to be at ease and engage positively with those who have additional needs. For example, on seeing Ella in her wheelchair regularly a parent responded by saying 'Isn't she sweet?' to her own child, seemingly not expecting any response or engagement. Her own child, after getting to know Ella as a playmate said insistently, 'No, Mummy, this is Ella, come and say hello.'

Practitioners worry about their conversations with parents where they highlight concerns about developmental progress. However, if the relationships are based on:

Respecting each other

- every interaction is based on caring professional relationships and respectful acknowledgement of the feelings of children and their families

Parents as partners

- parents are children's first and most enduring educators. When parents and practitioners work together in early years settings, the results have a positive impact on children's development and learning

Supporting learning

- warm trusting relationships with knowledgeable adults support children's learning more effectively than any amount of resources

These points were illustrated in the EYFS (Principle into Practice cards) (DfES 2007). Such relationships will demonstrate trust and honesty in every interaction enabling even difficult topics to be explored. It is impossible to know how a parent may feel about their child's special educational needs being identified and most parents report going through a range of emotions and responses. As we saw in the case studies, practitioners who can tune into parents' communication and recognize the need for both practical and emotional support make a real difference to parents' lives. Chapter 8 offered insights into parents' perspectives of how their children's needs have been met, including their experiences of early years provision. Not all were positive, reflecting considerable variation in practice. The joy and relief communicated in the descriptions of engagement with practitioners who really do embody the EYFS principles are palpable.

A way forward?

With all the frustrations and imperfect systems, practitioners still identify real positives in working with children with special educational needs. These include:

- an increased awareness of all children's learning, and development needs
- knowing more about the local services that are available so they can get help effectively for children
- the honing of early identification skills so they can more accurately recognize SEN and employ appropriate strategies in response
- finding ways to encourage other children to be socially engaged with a child with SEN as modelled by the adults in the setting

- developing good, respectful relationships with parents, recognizing them as individuals
- the importance of getting to know individual parents well enough to offer most appropriate support
- preparing the ground more effectively in the early stages of getting to know all parents and appropriately talking through differences in opinion, not just assuming that practitioners know best

We are increasingly aware of young children's brain development and the impact of early experience that makes each one of us unique. As we develop our skills, understanding and knowledge in working with children with special educational needs and disabilities, we cannot but improve our competence in working with all children. We influence each child's start in life and learning but we also impact on how parents interact and engage with professionals and whether they view us as supportive, distant or unhelpful.

As Ecaterina, Anya's mother, stated: 'Everywhere she has gone, Anya has made friends, as adults we show children how to interact with each other. This is highlighted even more when children have special needs, if we demonstrate everyone is part of the community like at the nursery, we create a community that includes all children.'

Our journey from the historical perspective to the present day has included examining different perspectives and experiences of special educational needs in early years settings. There is evidence of very skilled, high quality practice but also cumbersome systems and processes that have not always been helpful to families or practitioners. Throughout the historical review we can see a theme of increasing inclusion and a responsiveness of policy to children's and families' needs.

Indeed, the Plowden Report (HMSO 1967: 78) recommendations resonate strongly with recent debates calling for early identification, inter-agency collaboration, more sensitive and responsive support for those with disabilities, as well as more training for professionals. This was also echoed in the Warnock Report suggesting that all children should have a common educational experience responsive to their individual needs (HMSO 1978: 6). The statutory assessment process and the Statement of Special Educational Needs were intended to legally secure this ideal for children with special educational needs and disabilities. However, like the approaches to safeguarding, criticized by Munro, perhaps it was the rigidity of the SEN system that undermined its potential (Munro 2011: 60). As Mary Warnock herself said, 'The desire to "include" children in single institutions is a desire to treat them as the same, and, although a worthy ideal, can be carried too far. For children are also different, and it is essential to acknowledge this, since refusal to address genuine differences can wholly undermine our attempts to meet children's needs' (Warnock and Norwich 2010: 13).

There is no doubt, though, that progress has been made, since the Warnock Report spoke out against the segregation and discrimination endemic at the time. Three decades later we have concluded the issues are not simply about 'abled' and 'disabled' but about individual difference, and legislation has ultimately begun to reflect this change of thinking. As a result of advances in technology and research, our understanding of child development and special educational needs is deepening. The journey from segregation to inclusion is certainly progressing in terms of policy. Building on the UN Rights of the Child (1990), the UNESCO Salamanca Statement and the Equality Act 2010, the Children and Families Act (2014) affirms the importance of supporting children to 'achieve the best possible educational and other outcomes'. It also expressly puts children and their families at the heart of decision-making, encourages inclusive practice, and supports removing barriers to learning (HMSO 2014: 19).

In summary, we have consistent policy supporting the view that children have the right to educational opportunities that are flexible enough to meet their individual needs. This expressly includes children with special educational needs and disabilities and the expectation that, wherever possible, this will be in an inclusive mainstream provision. In January 2013 some 18% (1.55 million) of pupils in primary and secondary schools were identified as having special educational needs, whilst some 3% (229,390) had a statement and, of those with statements only 40% attended specialist provision (DfE 2013b: 3). The idea of a continuum of provision may indeed become more flexible if the EHC Plans are used creatively and practitioners are encouraged to work more collaboratively across the mainstream/special divide.

In the EYFS there is an inclusive, principled approach based on the premise that 'every child deserves the best possible start in life and the support that enables them to fulfil their potential' (DfE 2014: 5). Children are recognized from birth as competent learners, and their individual differences are acknowledged in the principle of the Unique Child. It is fair then to assert that high quality EYFS practice, as described in the statutory framework, encompasses early identification of children's needs and early intervention to support those needs. In this regard the SEND Code of Practice and the EYFS are complementary. However, as several recent reports have confirmed, it is the quality of provision that has been shown to be the crucial factor in making a difference to children's lives (Sylva et al. 2010; Smith et al. 2009; Mathers et al. 2014). Whilst individual practitioners can, and do, provide quality care for children, as Mathers et al. state, to consistently 'deliver high quality pedagogy, practitioners need to be skilled and knowledgeable and to work in environments which support them in their practice'. Without strong leadership and a common purpose individual practitioners are unlikely to be able to sustain high quality practice. Children with special educational needs and disabilities challenge us to improve our practice for all children and the SENCO is an important conduit for facilitating the learning of adults as well as of children.

The Children's Commissioner for England, Maggie Anderson, stated in the *Parliamentary Inquiry into Childcare for Disabled Children* that:

> Disabled children and young people have the right to enjoy the same opportunities as non-disabled children. This includes the right to local childcare and early learning opportunities, and to receive the support they need to fulfil their potential and to be involved in their communities.
>
> (Contact a Family 2014: 4)

Some key factors emerge in the report with 33% of parents citing lack of experienced staff as their reason for not accessing childcare. Their concerns included:

- lack of expertise, skills, or confidence in the workforce to include children with SEN and disabilities in their setting
- inflexibility in times when childcare is available in relation to family commitments
- family finance, with the cost of bringing up a child with disabilities three times more than that for a child without disability

The report also explores the vulnerability of families with children who have disabilities and how poverty due to additional costs and barriers to employment for parents is a reality for families (Contact a Family 2014: 9, 11). Introducing personal budgets as proposed in the Child Care Act (2014) with details included in EHC Plans is a step in the right direction, but in early years most children will not yet have such a plan. For families of children with special needs, their finances need to be considered holistically, taking account of reduced opportunities for employment and the increased costs involved in meeting a child's needs as well as flexible childcare and realistic short breaks.

Providers too can incur additional costs particularly related to building adaptations, ratios, staff training and specialist resources. The SEND Code of Practice requires local authorities to ensure that funding arrangements for all providers reflect the need to provide for children with special educational needs or disabilities. The local offer will no doubt provide the detail but local variation may create yet another frustration for practitioners and parents alike. The hope is that the recommended cross-party review of funding mechanisms related to inclusive childcare provision is alert to these complexities (Contact a Family 2014: 9, 21, 44).

Exploration of the parallel histories of SEN and early years education and care reveals the common purpose of meeting each child's needs where, as Margaret Hodge suggested, keeping the child is the central priority

(Gaunt 2014). Perhaps the next stage in this journey from segregation needs to be more inclusive, to go beyond the boundaries of thinking in terms of special educational needs and disabilities to consider the needs of all vulnerable learners.

In our increasing understanding about the factors which affect children's learning, perhaps we can extend the ideas of early identification and early intervention to include those whose learning may be compromised by poverty, abuse, neglect and parenting capacity. The Common Assessment Framework (CAF) or Early Help model is currently used in a variety of ways in local authorities to address such concerns but lack of clarity in practitioners about its purpose drastically reduces its effectiveness. The central intention must be to enable a holistic understanding of the child and their family.

As shown in Figure 10.1, using the overarching description of 'vulnerable learners' can help here by bringing together existing elements to complement each other and offer a cohesive approach to early identification and intervention. The links between the elements though need to be more explicit and at the forefront of practitioners' thinking. Supporting children with special needs and/or disabilities (SEND) should not be a 'bolt-on' option but

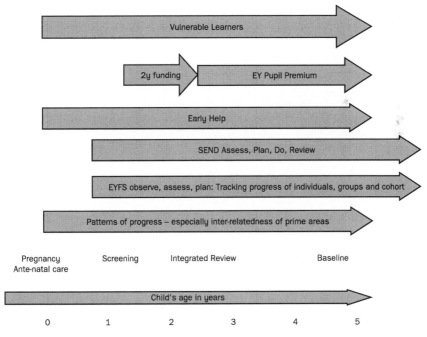

Figure 10.1: Using the overarching description of 'vulnerable learners' shows how existing elements supporting early identification and intervention can provide a cohesive and holistic approach

rather a central tenet of high quality practice. Indeed, if we truly believe that the EYFS really is a sure foundation for children's future success, we cannot handpick when it should or should not apply.

Connecting this strategic view to the daily experience of children, their families and practitioners, requires a belief in inclusion that goes beyond a child simply attending early years provision. We need to widen our use of the term 'inclusion' to ensure that a secure EYFS experience is a protective factor in all children's lives and one that enables their learning and development. Three decades after her significant contribution to special educational needs reform, encompassed in the Education Act of 1981, Mary Warnock publicly reassessed the idea of special educational needs. Her insights offer a simple challenge that communicates the essence of our common purpose in EYFS in meeting the needs of individual children, and recognizing and supporting the Unique Child.

Appendix 1

Running a multi-professional review meeting, prompt sheet

- Who would parents/practitioners like to be there?
- What are our realistic expectations about who will be able to attend?
- What different ways can we invite contributions to be submitted?
- What evidence and information is it relevant for us to communicate?

  - before the meeting
  - at the meeting
  - after the meeting

- What are the jobs which need to be done on the day?

  - taking notes
  - time keeping
  - welcoming and introductions
  - summarizing and agreeing actions, responsibilities and time-scales

- What do we understand to be the current situation regarding progress and challenges?
- What do we see as the important/ideal outcomes from the discussion? Including,

  - What needs to happen next?
  - What would be most helpful?

    - next week
    - next month
    - next year

- What significant events and decision-making opportunities are in the near future? For example,
  - 2-year check
  - medical appointments
  - transitions between rooms/settings

- What do we need to do to prepare?
  - make contact with others
  - clarify relevant information and expectations
  - explore the relevant 'local offer'

- When do we need to meet again? Why?

Appendix 2

Sample invitation to a review meeting

Please reply to: email   phone

Child's name   DOB

Parents' names

Setting name and address

Key Person's name

SENCO's name

XXXX's parents have asked that we invite you to contribute to his/her progress review meeting being held:

Date

Time

Venue:

If you are unable to attend in person, please respond in one of the following ways to let us know what progress you are aware of and what involvement you expect to have with the family over the next 6 months:

- Direct contact with names of mother and father
- Email to parents and/or setting
- Phone (the best time to contact the setting would be _____)
- Letter/report by post

We will ensure a copy of the meeting notes are sent to you once the meeting has taken place. If you would like to visit the setting or speak to us, please do get in touch once parents' permission has been confirmed.

Appendix 3

Prime Areas tracking progress: Darren 10 months old

See Chapter 5 for more information about Darren

Darren 10 months old	Birth to 11 months	8–20 months	16–26 months	22–36 months	30–50 months	40–60 months
PSED Making relationships						
Self-confidence and self-awareness						
Managing feelings and behaviour						
CL Listening and attention						
Understanding						
Speaking						
PD Moving and handling						
Health and Self-Care						

This tracking sheet is an overview of the Key Person's and SENCO's assessments of Darren's progress at 10 months old, based on their observations and discussions with his parents. It indicates that overall his progress is in line with typical development at this time.

Prime areas tracking progress: Darren 20 months old

Darren 20 months	Birth to 11 months	8–20 months	16–26 months	22–36 months	30–50 months	40–60 months
PSED Making relationships	▓					
Self-confidence and self-awareness	▓					
Managing feelings and behaviour	▓					
CL Listening and attention	▓	▓				
Understanding	▓	▓				
Speaking	▓					
PD Moving and handling	▓					
Health and Self-Care	▓					
	▓					

Ten months on from the previous overview sheet we see that Darren has made progress in two aspects of communication and language. This pattern of progress triggered the Key Person and SENCO exploring with Darren's parents possible reason why he might not have made as much progress in the other prime areas.

Prime areas tracking progress: Darren up to 47 months old

10 months	20 months	30 months	47 months

Darren 47 months	Birth to 11 months	8–20 months	16–26 months	22–36 months	30–50 months	40–60 months
PSED Making relationships						
Self-confidence and self-awareness						
Managing feelings and behaviour						
CL Listening and attention						
Understanding						
Speaking						
PD Moving and handling						
Health and Self-Care						

By 47 months Darren had made significant progress in response to interventions implemented by his Key Person. These interventions were contributed to and supported by his parents, the physio and speech and language therapists as well as the SENCO. Darren's subsequent referral to a paediatrician led to a diagnosis of a rare genetic condition particularly affecting his physical development.

Appendix 4

Sample play plan for Darren (format devised by J. Darkes-Sutcliffe)

This is me	My name is Darren James I was born on: 21 May 2010 Today's date is: 13 May 2012
	At the moment I really like: When Mum sings 'Twinkle, Twinkle' and cuddles with my special people. 'Tummy time' on the blue soft mat with different textured things around me to attract my interest.
	At the moment I really dislike: When someone puts me in a position where I cannot see any of my special people or reach interesting things to explore.
	I am interested in: Different textures of things in my treasure basket especially, shiny, soft, hard and rough.
	I am good at: Letting people know if I am happy or uncomfortable. I have a special gurgling noise which tells people when I am really happy, all my special people know this noise. They smile and cuddle me when I make it.
	My next steps in learning: To sit unsupported in the cosy corner for one minute while playing with my treasure basket.
EYFS and Development Matters links: Prime areas: PD, CL and PSED are as described in age band Birth to 11 months	Resources and activities likely to help my learning: Identifying different opportunities in familiar daily routines and activities to encourage me to use my muscles. Such as: nappy changing, stretching during tummy time, getting dressed, reaching for my toes, etc.

People who help me learn at home and in the setting:

Mum, Dad, Granny, Bob, Mandy, Gemma and Jamila.

My thinking about my play plan is that:

People know what I like.

You can look at what I have been doing in my folder which is kept .... in my room box

This play plan will be reviewed on: 12 June 2013

These people have been involved in this discussion about my learning and development today:

Tariq, Jackie, Mandy and Jamila.

Actions agreed	By whom	By when
• To make changes to daily routines to enable Darren to use his muscles more	Jackie, Tariq and Mandy	15 May
• To seek advice from the specialist Early Years team at the Children's Centre about specific ways to help with early physical development	Mandy and Tariq	15 May
• To ask for suggestions of suitable activities to support Darren and any additional sources of advice at the next SENCO Network meeting	Jamila	28 May

Blank play plan format 1

This is me	My name is:	I was born on:	Today's date is:
	At the moment I really like:		
	At the moment I really dislike:		
	I am interested in:		
	I am good at:		
	My next steps in learning:		
EYFS and Development Matters links: Prime areas: PD, CL and PSED are as described in age band Birth to 11 months	Resources and activities likely to help my learning:		

People who help me learn at home and in the setting:

My thinking about my play plan is that:

You can look at what I have been doing in my folder which is kept ....
This play plan will be reviewed on:
These people have been involved in this discussion about my learning and development today:

Actions agreed	By whom	By when

Appendix 5

Blank play plan format 2: Assess, Plan, Do, Review followed by completed sample plan for Peter who appears in Chapter 9

Name:	DOB	Today's date:	Play plan number:
		Information update	
Things I enjoy doing:		Things I do not like:	
People I like being with:		People I don't like being with:	
I can now:		I would like to:	
Key information from home (*summarize and prioritize views, changes, concerns, etc. into approx. 3 bullet points*)			
Key information from setting (*summarize and prioritize views, changes, concerns, etc. into approx. 3 bullet points*)			
Key information from other services (*summarize and prioritize views, changes, concerns, etc. into approx. 3 bullet points*)			

Assess

Think about:
What more have we learned about how _____ approaches his learning and making sense of the world since the last review?
What impact have we seen of current strategies and interventions?
Was the rate of progress typical for _____ or accelerated by these interventions?
What could we do, at home and in the settings to further support _____, learning and development?
Where beyond the setting might we access helpful information and/or support?

Using the information and evidence available we assess:
> *the most effective form of support at this time for _____ is:*

> *the priorities for learning and development (consider especially progress in the EYFS Prime Areas) at this time are:*

> *sources of information that have been used to inform our thinking (e.g. Development Matters, Child Development information, specialist information, local authority local offer)*

Plan

Learning and development:
Next step 1:

Learning and development:
Next step 2:

How will adults help to give me the best possible chance to take my next steps?
(include details of interventions which are additional to and different from those for the majority of children)

	Do
The adults who devised this plan were:	These adults also need to know about this plan:

Actions agreed	By whom	By when

Review

Date of next review:

Consider:

What progress has been made?
What was the specific impact of the interventions?

Why was it not more?
What else could we do?

Why was it more than we expected?
Where else could we go for help and advice?

Play Plan completed example for Peter

Name: Peter	DOB 21/1/10	Today's date: 15/3/14	Play Plan number: 6
		Information update	
Things I enjoy doing: Being outside in the den, counting things, putting all the cars in the garage, inset jigsaw puzzles		Things I do not like: Unexpected noises, any loud noises, fruit or soft squishy food like jelly or sponge cakes	
People I like being with:		People I don't like being with:	
At home: Mum, Dad, Jeana, Billy At Nursery: adults: Maureen, Janine, Yvonne Children: Hamsa, Charlie, Milly, Patrice		At nursery: adults: Penny, Shima Children: Joshua, Jamal	
I can now:		I would like to:	
Play alongside Charlie, Milly and Hamsa when Maureen is with me Use signs for: more, thumbs up Recognize phrases: 'Are you ready?', 'Next one', and 'Thank you, Peter' Complete the 5-piece inset puzzles (animal and vehicle sets)		Join Charlie, Milly and Hamsa play independently Feel less upset by noises	
Key information from home (*summarize and prioritize views, changes, concerns, etc. into approx. 3 bullet points*)			
Tatu had a useful conversation with Adrian (SALT) and will be using Makaton at home with Peter Peter is still not sleeping through the night but is more relaxed about coming to nursery Panya and Tatu feel that Peter's reaction to loud noises is causing most distress at the moment			

Assess

Think about:
What more have we learned about how _____Peter_____ approaches his learning and making sense of the world since the last review?
What impact have we seen of current strategies and interventions?
Was the rate of progress typical for _____Peter_ or accelerated by these interventions?
What could we do, at home and in the setting, to further support _____Peter's_____ learning and development?
Where beyond the setting might we access helpful information and/or support?

Using the information and evidence available we assess:
the most effective form of support at this time for _____Peter_____ is:

targeted Key Person time twice per day, before lunch and before home time
using activities where he is most relaxed to introduce new learning/strategies
new learning, key phrases, etc. supported by all practitioners throughout the day
using same key phrases/signing at home and nursery

linking approaches to next steps with usual routines at home
the priorities for learning and development (consider especially progress in the EYFS Prime Areas) at this time are:

PSED – dealing with emotions especially anxiety related to loud noises
CL – extending verbal and signing
PD – exploring food textures in cooking activities

sources of information that have been used to inform our thinking
(e.g. Development Matters, Child Development information, specialist information, local authority local offer)

Development Matters to support conversations with Tatu, Panya and Adrian (SALT)
National Strategies Inclusion Development Programme: Supporting Children on the Autistic Spectrum
Rainbow Room information booklet (produced by local ASD unit practitioners)
SENCO Forum sessions related to ASD in early years
Autism in Early Years book (Kate Wall, 2004)

Plan

Learning and development:
Next step 1:
To take turns with Maureen to complete a 5-piece inset puzzle

Learning and development:
Next step 2:
To be able to tolerate sounds in games and books when I make them happen

How will adults help to give me the best possible chance to take my next steps?
(include details of interventions which are additional to and different from those for the majority of children)
At home:
Use Peter's favourite story such as his farm animal jigsaw book, encourage him to make noises for the animals
Keep using: 'Are you ready?', 'Next one', and 'Thank you, Peter' in appropriate contexts
At Nursery:
Begin doing activities in 1:1 session in separate room then move to open area
Use animal and vehicle puzzle sets
Use the vehicle sound book with buttons Peter can press to make the noise

Key information from setting *(summarize and prioritize views, changes, concerns, etc. into approx. 3 bullet points)*

Recent observations show:
Peter making approaches to join others' play – his strategy is to stand very close then try to take the toy/puzzle they are using
If there is a loud unexpected noise, Peter is upset for approx. 10 minutes afterwards
Peter is recognizing and responding consistently to 2 signs and 3 key phrases

Key information from other services (*summarize and prioritize views, changes, concerns, etc. into approx. 3 bullet points*)

SALT:

Adrian has provided a list of Makaton signs and symbol cards to use for Peter, in addition to those already on display in nursery

Peter's receptive language is more evident and increasing now that he is more relaxed in nursery

Adrian suggests that opportunities to encourage 1:1 turn taking should be identified and increased

Paediatrician:

The next appointment is in June so reports/play plans need to be collated and reviewed to update the Paediatrician with Peter's progress

Early Years Team: Janine met Tatu and Panya at nursery to talk about the LA local offer, information about local parent support groups, sources of information. Tatu and Panya want to meet Janine again in two weeks to talk about a future school place for Peter.

Do	
The adults who devised this plan were:	These adults also need to know about this plan:
Mother: Tatu Father: Panya Key Person: Maureen SENCO: Nadhu	Speech and Language Therapist: Adrian Early Years Team: Eloise

Actions agreed	By whom	By when
1. To provide copy of play plan for Tatu and Panya and the SALT	Nadhu	17/3/14
2. To begin using inset puzzles and sound book in 10-minute 1:1 session with Peter, just before lunch in the library.	Maureen	16/3/14

Review

Date of next review: 15th March (review of Play Plan 5)

Consider:

| What progress has been made? | Why was it not more? | Why was it more than we expected? |
| What was the specific impact of the interventions? | What else could we do? | Where else could we go for help and advice? |

- Peter has made more progress than expected in his willingness to engage with particular children, alongside Maureen and is beginning to use the sign for 'more' to communicate with them
- Peter is now able to tolerate playing alongside 3 other children consistently
- Choosing times when the children were playing with cars or in the den was most successful, we think this was because it was when Peter was most relaxed
- We now understand that Peter will choose and likes being with Charlie, Milly, Hamsa and Patrice. They also enjoy time with Peter when he is with them.
- A specific impact has been that Peter is showing more interest in what other children are doing, sometimes standing very close as if he wants to join in but this can result in him taking the toy they are playing with
- Peter now has an established routine of arriving at nursery, running round the room, outside, then finding Maureen and taking her to the activity he would like to do first. We think he is using this process to see what other children are doing and to find an activity he likes. After this first activity he will happily go to another activity without Maureen. Tatu and Panya recognize this pattern of response as similar to when they visited family and friends and Peter does a 'tour' of space indoors and out before he can settle
- Specific conversations with Tatu and Panya have helped us to recognize signs that Peter's anxiety is reducing in particular situations
- Eloise from the Early Years Team has suggested that Tatu and Panya visit the Rainbow Room (local ASD unit) and that we establish a link with the staff team too

Date of next review: 10th April

Consider:
What progress has been made?
What was the specific impact of the interventions?

Why was it not more?
What else could we do?

Why was it more than we expected?
Where else could we go for help and advice?

Bibliography

Abbott, L. and Rodger, R. (2000). *Quality Education in the Early Years.* Buckingham: Open University Press

Allard, A., Delamore, J. and Carlin, J. (eds) (2014). *Dignity and Inclusion: Making it work for children with complex health care needs.* London: National Children's Bureau

Allen, G. (ed.) (2011). *Early Intervention: The next steps.* London: Cabinet Office

Alliance for Inclusive Education (2013). How was school project: timeline. Available at www.allfie.org.uk

Armstrong, D. and Squires, G. (2012). *Contemporary Issues in Special Educational Needs: Considering the whole child.* Maidenhead: Open University Press

Astington, J.W. (1993). *The Child's Discovery of the Mind.* Cambridge, MA: Harvard University Press

Audit Commission (2002) *Special Educational Needs: A Mainstream Issue.* London: Audit Commission

Bennathan, M. and Boxall, M. (1998). *The Boxall Profile Handbook for Teachers.* The Nurture Group Network. Available at http://www.nurturegroups.org

Bird, S. and Rogers, M. (2010) *Early Intervention for Children and Families.* London: C4EO, Centre for Excellence and Outcomes in Children and Young People's Services

Birsch, K. H. (2011). *Treating Attachment Disorders*, 2nd edition. New York: The Guildford Press

Blades, R. and Kumari, V. (2011). *Putting Listening Practice at the Heart of Early Years Practice: An evaluation of the Young Children's Voices Network.* London: National Children's Bureau

Booker, L. and Woodhead, M. (2007). *Early Childhood in Focus 2: Transitions in the lives of young children.* Milton Keynes: The Open University Press

Booker, L. and Woodhead, M. (2008). *Early Childhood in Focus 3: Developing positive identities*. Milton Keynes: The Open University Press

Booker, L. and Woodhead, M. (2010). *Early Childhood in Focus 6: Culture and learning*. Milton Keynes: The Open University Press

Boyle, C. and Topping, K. (eds) (2012). *What Works in Inclusion?* Maidenhead: Open University Press

British Journal of Nursing (1926). *Royal Commission on Lunacy and Mental Disorder.* Available at http://rcnarchive.rcn.org.uk/data/VOLUME074–1926/page200-volume74-september1926.pdf] [accessed 13 Nov. 2013]

Brownell, C.A and Kopp, C.B. (eds) (2007). *Socioemotional Development in the Toddler Years: Transitions and transformations*. New York: The Guildford Press

Cabinet Office (2010). *The Foundation Years: Preventing poor children becoming poor adults*. London: HMSO

Carpendale, J., and Lewis, C. (2006). *How Children Develop Social Understanding*. Oxford: Blackwell Publishing

Children's Workforce Development Council (2006) *Early Identification, Assessment of Needs and Intervention: The Common Assessment Framework*. Leeds: CWDC

Clark, A. (2011). *Listening as a Way of Life*. Young Children's Voices Network. London: National Children's Bureau

Contact a Family (2013). *Relationships and Caring for a Disabled Child*. London. Available at www.contactafamily.org [accessed August 2014]

Contact a Family (2014). *Parliamentary Inquiry into childcare for disabled children*. London. Available at: www.contactafamily.org [accessed August 2014]

Cook, J. (2013). *Leadership and Management in the Early Years*. London: Practical Pre-school Books

Davis, H. and Day, C. (2007). *Current Family Partnership Model*. London: South London and Maudsley NHS Foundation Trust

DeCasper and Spence in Ward, J. (2010). Cited in *The Student's Guide to Social Neuroscience*. London: Psychology Press

Department for Children, Schools and Families (2009). Inclusion Development Programme: Supporting Children with Behavioural, Social and Emotional Difficulties: guidance for practitioners in the early years foundation stage, London, DCSF. http://www.foundationyears.org.uk/?s=inclusion+development+programme

Department for Children, Schools and Families (2009). Inclusion Development Programme: Supporting Children on the autism spectrum: guidance for practitioners in the early years foundation stage, London, DCSF. http://www.foundationyears.org.uk/?s=inclusion+development+programme

Department for Children, Schools and Families (2009). *Inclusion Development Programme: Supporting Children with speech, language and communication needs: guidance for practitioners in the early years foundation stage*, London, DCSF. http://www.foundationyears.org.uk/ ?s=inclusion+development+programme

Department for Education (1999). *The National Curriculum: Handbook for primary teachers in England*. London: DfE

Department for Education (1999a). *Good Practice for EYDC Partnerships: Developing and supporting high quality, sustainable childcare*. London: DfE

Department for Education (2011). *Support and Aspiration: A new approach to special educational needs and disability*. London: DfE

Department for Education (2011a). *The Early Years: Foundations for life, health and learning*. London: DfE

Department for Education (2011b). *Munro Review of Child Protection*. Available at: www.education.org.uk

Department for Education (2012). *A Profile of Pupil Exclusions in England. Education Standards Analysis and Research Division Research Report. DFE-RR190*. London: DfE

Department for Education (2012a). *Statutory Framework for the Early Years Foundation Stage: Setting the standards for learning, development and care for children from birth to five*. London. Available at: www.education.org.uk

Department for Education (2012b). *The Common Assessment Process*. Available at: www.education.org.uk

Department for Education (2013). *Early Years Outcomes*. Available at: www.education.org.uk

Department for Education (2013a). *Early Years Foundation Stage Profile: Handbook 2013*. London: DfE

Department for Education (2013b). *Statistical Release SFR 42/2013 Children with Special Educational Needs 2013: An analysis*. London: DfE, Chapter 1

Department for Education (2014). *Early Years Foundation Stage Profile: Handbook 2014*. London: DfE

Department for Education (2014a). *Special Educational Needs and Disability Code of Practice: 0 to 25 years*. London: DfE

Department for Education and Department of Health (2014a). *Draft Special Educational Needs (SEN) Code of Practice: For 0 to 25 years*. London: DfE

Department for Education and Employment (1997). *Excellence for All Children: Meeting special educational needs*. Available at: www.education-england.org.uk [accessed January 2014]

Department for Education and Skills (2001). *Ofsted National Standards*. London: Ofsted

Department for Education and Skills (2001a). *Special Educational Needs Code of Practice*. London: DfES

Department for Education and Skills (2003). *Every Child Matters*. London: DfES

Department for Education and Skills (2003a) *Birth to Three Matters*. London: DfES/Sure Start

Department for Education and Skills (2004). *Removing Barriers to Achievement: The government's strategy for SEN*. London: DfES

Department for Education and Skills (2006). *Including Me: Managing complex health needs in schools and early years settings*: Council for Disabled Children. London: National Children's Bureau

Department for Education and Skills (2007). *Statutory Framework for the Early Years Foundation Stage (EYFS)*. London: DfES

Department for Education and Skills/Qualifications, Curriculum and Assessment Authority (2000). *Curriculum Guidance for the Foundation Stage*. London: DfE

Department of Health (2009). *The Healthy Child Programme*. London: DoH

Department of Health (2011). *The Health Visitor Implementation Plan*. London: DoH

Department of Work and Pensions (2012). *Child Poverty in the UK: The report on the 2010 target*. London. Available at: www.official-documents. gov.uk [accessed December 2013]

Disability Rights Commission (2002). *Code of Practice for Schools Disability Discrimination Act 1995*. London: The Stationery Office

Dorman, H. and Dorman, C. (2002). *The Social Toddler*. Surrey: CP Publishing

Dowling, M. (2005). *Young Children's Personal, Social and Emotional Development*. London: Paul Chapman Publishing

Dunn, J. (2004). *Children's Friendships: The beginnings of intimacy*. Oxford: Blackwell Publishing

Dyson, A. with Alan Millward, Deanne Crowther, John Elliott and Ian Hall. (2002). *Research Report 248: Decision-making and provision within the framework of the SEN Code of Practice*. Newcastle: University of Newcastle, Special Needs Research Centre

Early Education (2012). *Development Matters in the Early Years Foundation Stage (EYFS)*. London: Early Education

Early Support (2006). *Participants' Pre-Course Handout on the Family Partnership Model*. London: National Children's Bureau

Easton, C., Lamont, L., Smith, R. and Aston, H. (2013). '*We Should Have Been Helped from Day One': A unique perspective from children, families and practitioners. Findings from LARC5*. Slough: NFER

Egan, G. (1982). *The Skilled Helper*. 2nd edition. Belmont, CA: Wadsworth

Elfer, P., Goldschmied, E. and Selleck, D.Y. (2012). *Key Persons in the Early Years: Building relationships for quality provision in early years settings and primary schools*. London: Routledge

English Heritage (2013). *Disability History*. Available at http: //www.english-heritage.org.uk/discover/people-and-places/disability-history/1914–1945/ [accessed August 2013]

Evangelou, M., Sylva, K., Kyriacou, M., Wild, M. and Glenny, G. (2009). *Early Years Learning and Development: Literature Review*. London: Department for Children, Schools and Families

Evans, K., George, N., White, K., Sharp, C., Morris, M. and Marshall, H. (2010). *Ensuring that all Children and Young People Make Sustained Progress and Remain Fully Engaged through all Transitions Between Key Stages* (C4EO Schools and Communities Research Review 2). London: Centre for Excellence and Outcomes in Children and Young People's Services

Farrell, M. (2004). *Special Educational Needs: A resource for practitioners*. London: Paul Chapman Publishing

Freud, S. (1950). *Totem and Taboo*. London: Routledge and Kegan Paul

Further Education Funding Council (1994). *National Vocational Qualifications in the Further Education Sector in England*. Coventry: DfES

Garrett, B. (2009). *Brain and Behaviour*. London: Sage Publications

Gaunt, C. (2014). Margaret Hodge urges slow down on two-year-old expansion. *Nursery World*, 4 June

Gerhardt, S. (2004). *Why Love Matters*. Hove: Routledge

Gillard, D. (2011). *Education in England: A brief history*. Available at: www.educationengland.org.uk/history [accessed May–December 2013]

Goldschmied, E. and Jackson, S. (1994). *People Under Three: Young children in day care*. London: Routledge

Goouch, K. and Powell, S. (2013). *The Baby Room: Principles, policy and practice*. Maidenhead: Open University Press

Great Britain Commission (1908). *Report of the Royal Commission on the Care and Control of the Feebleminded*. Available at: https: //archive.org/details/reportroyalcomm00mindgoog [accessed 14 July 2013]

Hala, S. (ed.) (1997). *The Development of Social Cognition*. Hove: Psychology Press

Hallett, F. and Hallet, G. (eds) (2010). *Transforming the Role of the SENCO*. Maidenhead: Open University Press

Hallett, C. and Prout, A. (2003). *Hearing the Voices of Children: Social policy for a new century*. London: Routledge

Harris, A. and Goodall, J. (2007). *Engaging Parents in Raising Achievement – Do parents know they matter?* Department for Education and Skills Research Brief DCSF-RBW004. London: DfES

Herbert, M. (2003). *Typical and Atypical Development*. Oxford: Blackwell

HMSO (Her Majesty's Stationery Office) (1902). *Education Act 1902.* London: HMSO

HMSO (Her Majesty's Stationery Office) (1908). *Education Act 1908.* London: HMSO

HMSO (Her Majesty's Stationery Office) (1913). *The Mental Deficiency Act 1913.* London: HMSO

HMSO (Her Majesty's Stationery Office) (1933). *The Hadow Report: Infant and nursery schools.* London: HMSO

HMSO (Her Majesty's Stationery Office) (1944). *Disabled Persons (Employment) Act, 1944.* London: HMSO

HMSO (Her Majesty's Stationery Office) (1944a). *The Education Act (1944).* London: HMSO

HMSO (Her Majesty's Stationery Office) (1948). *National Assistance Act.* London: HMSO

HMSO (Her Majesty's Stationery Office) (1948a). *Nurseries and Childminders Regulation Act.* London: HMSO

HMSO (Her Majesty's Stationery Office) (1959). *Mental Health Act 1959.* London. Available at: http: //www.legislation.gov.uk/ukpga/Eliz2/7–8/72/ contents [accessed 20 Aug. 2013]

HMSO (Her Majesty's Stationery Office) (1967). *The Plowden Report,* Vol. 1, London: HMSO

HMSO (Her Majesty's Stationery Office) (1968). *The Summerfield Report.* London: HMSO

HMSO (Her Majesty's Stationery Office) (1970). *Chronically Sick and Disabled Persons Act 1970.* London: HMSO

HMSO (Her Majesty's Stationery Office) (1970a). *The Education (Handicapped Children) Act.* London: HMSO

HMSO (Her Majesty's Stationery Office) (1978). *Special Educational Needs.* London: HMSO

HMSO (Her Majesty's Stationery Office) (1988). *Education Reform Act.* London: HMSO

HMSO (Her Majesty's Stationery Office) (1989). *The Children's Act.* London: HMSO

HMSO (Her Majesty's Stationery Office) (1989a). Her Majesty's Inspectorate (HMI) Aspects of Primary Education series *The Education of Children Under Five,* London: HMSO

HMSO (Her Majesty's Stationery Office) (1990). *Starting with Quality.* London: HMSO

HMSO (Her Majesty's Stationery Office) (1992). *Education (Schools) Act 1992.* London: HMSO

HMSO (Her Majesty's Stationery Office) (1993). *Education Act 1993.* London: HMSO

HMSO (Her Majesty's Stationery Office) (1995). *Disability Discrimination*

HMSO (Her Majesty's Stationery Office) (1996). *Nursery Education and Grant-Maintained Schools Act 1995.* London: HMSO

HMSO (Her Majesty's Stationery Office) (1997). *White Paper: Excellence in Schools.* London: HMSO

HMSO (Her Majesty's Stationery Office) (1998). *Education Reform Act.* London: HMSO

HMSO (Her Majesty's Stationery Office) (1998a). *Schools Standards and Framework Act 1998.* London: HMSO

HMSO (Her Majesty's Stationery Office) (2000). *The Care Standards Act 2000.* London: HMSO

HMSO (Her Majesty's Stationery Office) (2001). *Special Educational Needs and Disability Act 2001,* London: HMSO

HMSO (Her Majesty's Stationery Office) (2002). *Education Act 2002.* London: HMSO

HMSO (Her Majesty's Stationery Office) (2003). *Green Paper: Every Child Matters.* London: HMSO

HMSO (Her Majesty's Stationery Office) (2008). *Special Educational Needs (Information) Act 2008.* London: HMSO

HMSO (Her Majesty's Stationery Office) (2010). *Equality Act 2010.* London: HMSO

HMSO (Her Majesty's Stationery Office) (2010a). *Child Poverty Act 2010.* London: HMSO

HMSO (Her Majesty's Stationery Office) (2012). *Equality Act 2011.* London: HMSO

HMSO (Her Majesty's Stationery Office) (2012a). *Health and Social Care Act 2012.* London: HMSO

HMSO (Her Majesty's Stationery Office) (2013). *Children and Families Bill:* as amended at Grand Committee. London: HMSO

HMSO (Her Majesty's Stationery Office) (2014). *Children and Families Act.* London: HMSO

Hughes, C. (2011). *Social Understanding and Social Lives.* London: Psychology Press

Hunt, S. (2008). Controversies in treatment approaches: Gene therapy, IVF, stem cells, and pharmacogenomics. *Nature Education* 1(1): 222

Institute of Education (2009). *Archives Subject Guide No. 3.* London. Available at: www.ioe.ac.uk [accessed 24 Nov. 2013]

Inui, T. (2013). Toward a unified framework for understanding the various symptoms and etiology of autism and Williams syndrome. *Japanese Psychological Research* 55(2): 99–117. doi: 10.1111/jpr.12004

Judd, J. (1996). Schools cram in nursery voucher scheme children. *Independent* 14 November 1996. Available at: www.independent.co.uk [accessed

Labour Party (1994). *Opening Doors to a Learning Society: A policy statement on education.* Available at: www.educationengland.org.uk [accessed December 2013]

Laevers, F. (2000). Forward to basics! Deep-level learning and the experiential approach. *Early Years* 20(2): 20–9

Life Long Learning Programme (2010). *Professional Partnerships for Inclusive Education: An inclusive edcuation guide for professionals.* Available at: http://www.allfie.org.uk/pages/work/resources.html [accessed 2 Dec. 2013]

MacKinnon, D., Statham, J., with Hales, M. (1995). *Education in the UK: Facts and figures.* London: Open University Press/Hodder and Stoughton

Marmot, M. (2010). *The Marmot Review: Fair society, healthy lives.* London: University College London

Mathers, S. and Smees, R. (2014). *Quality and Inequality: Do three- and four-year-olds in deprived areas experience lower quality early years provision?* London: The Nuffield Foundation.

Mathieson, K. (2005). *Social Skills in the Early Years.* London: Paul Chapman Publishing

Mathieson, K. (2007). *Identifying Special Needs in the Early Years.* London: Paul Chapman Publishing

Mathieson, K. (2013). *I Am Two!: Working effectively with two year olds and their families.* London: The British Association for Early Childhood Education

Meins, E., Fernyhough, C., Wainwright, R., Gupta, M.D., Fradely, E. and Tuckey, M. (2002). Maternal mind-mindedness and attachment security as predictors of theory of mind understanding. *Child Development* 73(6): 1715–26

Melhuish, E., Belsky, J., MacPherson, K. and Cullis, A. (2010). *The Quality of Group Childcare Settings Used by 3–4 Year Old Children in Sure Start Local Programme Areas and the Relationship with Child Outcomes. Department of Education Research Report.* London: DfE.

Mortimer, H. (2001). *Special Needs and Early Years Provision.* London: Continuum

Moylett, H. and Stewart, N. (2013). *Emerging, Expected, Exceeding: Understanding the revised Foundation Stage Profile.* London: The British Association of Early Childhood Education

Munro, E. (2011). *The Munro Review of Child Protection: Interim Report – The Child's Journey.* London: TSO

National Children's Bureau (www.ncb.org.uk) (2013). Early Support resources. Available at: http://www.councilfordisabledchildren.org.uk/what-we-do/networks-campaigning/early-support [accessed August 2013]

National Children's Bureau (2013a). *A Know How Guide: The EYFS progress check at two.* Available at: https: //www.gov.uk/government/publications/ a-know-how-guide-the-eyfs-progress-check-at-age-two.

National Health Service (2013). *The History of the NHS in England.* Available at: http://www.nhs.uk/NHSEngland/thenhs/nhshistory/Pages/ NHShistory1948.aspx [accessed 21 August 2013]

National Institute for Health and Care Excellence (2013). *Autism: The management and support of children and young people on the autism spectrum.* Manchester: NICE

Norwich, B. (2008). *Dilemmas of Difference, Inclusion and Disability: International perspective and future directions.* London: Routledge.

Norwich, B. (2013). *Addressing Tensions and Dilemmas in Education: Living with uncertainty.* London: Routledge

Nutbrown, C. (2006). *Key Concepts in Early Childhood Education and Care.* London: Sage Publications

Nutbrown, C. and Clough, P. (2006). *Inclusion in the Early Years.* London: Sage Publications

Nutbrown, C., Clough, P. and Selbie, P. (2008). *Early Childhood Education: History, Philosophy and Experience.* London: Sage Publications

Nutbrown, C., Clough, P. and Selbie, P. (2010). *Early Childhood Education: History, philosophy and experience.* London: Sage Publications

Oates, J., Karmiloff-Smith, A. and Johnson, M.H. (eds) (2012). *Early Childhood in Focus 7: Developing brains.* Milton Keynes: The Open University Press

O'Brien, T. (ed.) (2002). *Enabling Inclusion: Blue skies . . . dark clouds?* London: Optimus Publishing

Office of National Statistics (2011). *UK Census Data.* Available at: www.ons. gov.uk [accessed 4 November 2013]

Parker, I. (2013). *Early Developments: Bridging the gap between evidence and policy in early-years education.* London: IPPR, Institute for Public Policy Research

Pray, L. (2008). Discovery of DNA structure and function: Watson and Crick. *Nature Education* 1(1): 100. Available at: http://www.nature.com/ scitable/topicpage/discovery-of-dna-structure-and-function- watson–397 [accessed 28 February 2014]

Pre-school Learning Alliance (2013). *Our History.* Available at: https://www. pre-school.org.uk/about-us/history [accessed 23 August 2013]

Public Record Office of Northern Ireland (2007). Ministry/Department of Education Archive. Available at: http://www.proni.gov.uk/introduction _education_archive–2.pdf [accessed August 2013]

Pugh, G. (ed.) (2001). *Contemporary Issues in the Early Years 3rd edition.* London: Paul Chapman

Pugh, G. and Duffy, B. (eds) (2006). *Contemporary Issues in the Early Years, 4th edition*. London: Sage

Pugh, G. and Duffy, B. (eds) (2014). *Contemporary Issues in the Early Years, Sixth Edition*. London: Sage

Qualifications, Curriculum and Assessment Authority (2000). *Curriculum Guidance for the Foundation Stage*. London: QCA

Qualifications, Curriculum and Assessment Authority (2005). *Seeing Steps in Children's Learning*. London: QCA

Qualifications, Curriculum and Assessment Authority (2005a). *Building the Profile*. London: QCA

Roberts, K. (2009). *Early Home Learning Matters*. Available at: www.family andparenting.org

Robinson, M. (2003). *Birth to One*. Buckingham: Open University Press

Rogers, B. and McPherson, E. (2008). *Behaviour Management with Young Children*. London: Sage Publications Ltd

Rogoff, B. (2003). *The Cultural Nature of Human Development*. Oxford: Oxford University Press

Rose, J. and Rogers, S. (2012). *The Role of the Adult in Early Years Settings*. Maidenhead: Open University Press

Sammons, P., Smees, R., Taggart, B., Sylva, K., Melhuish, E., Siraj-Blatchford, I. and Elliot, K. (2003). *Technical Paper 1: Special Education Needs across the Pre-school Period*. London: Institute of Education, University of London

Shonkoff, J.P. and Phillips, A. (eds) (2000). *From Neurons to Neighbourhoods*. Washington, DC: National Academy Press

Smith, R., Purdon, S., Mathers, S., Sylva, K., Schneider, V., et al. (2009). *Early Education Pilot for Two Year Old Children Evaluation*. DCSF Research Report RR134 London: TSO

Society for Neuroscience (SfN) (2012). *Brain Facts: A primer on the brain and nervous systems*. Available at: www.sfn.org

Stewart, N. (2011). *How Children Learn: The characteristics of effective early learning*. London: The British Association for Early Childhood Education.

Sure Start (2002). *Birth to Three Matters: A framework to support children in their earliest years*. Nottingham: Department of Education and Skills

Sure Start (2002a). *Getting Sure Start Started: National Evaluation of Sure Start (NESS)* Nottingham: Department of Education and Skills

Sure Start (2003). *Characteristics of Sure Start Local Programme Areas, Rounds 1 to 4*. Nottingham: Department of Education and Skills

Sylva, K., Melhuish, E., Sammons, P., Siraj-Blatchford, I. and Taggart, B. (eds) (2010). *Early Childhood Matters: Evidence from the effective pre-school and primary education project*. London: Routledge

Thalidomide Society (2013). Available at: www.thalidomidesociety.org

Thane, P. (2009). History and Policy: Connecting historians, policymakers and the media. Memorandum submitted to the House of Commons' health committee inquiry: Social Care. London: Centre for Contemporary British History

Trevarthen, C. (1993). The function of emotions in early infant communication and development. In J. Nadel and L. Camaioni (eds) *New Perspectives in Early Communicative Development*. London: Routledge

UNESCO (United Nations Educational, Scientific and Cultural Organisation) (1994). *The Salamanca Statement and Framework for Action on Special Needs Education*. Spain: Ministry of Education and Science

UNICEF (1990) Declaration of the Rights of the Child. Available at: http://www.unicef.org.uk/UNICEFs-Work/Our-mission/UN-Convention/ [accessed 18 Aug. 2013]

United Nations (1924). Declaration of the Rights of the Child. Available at: http://www.un-documents.net/gdrc1924.htm [accessed 18 Aug. 2013]

United Nations (1948). Declaration of Human Rights. Available at: http://www.un.org/en/documents/udhr/history.shtml [accessed 18 Aug. 2013]

Vargas-Silva, C. (2014). Long-term international migration flows to and from the UK. Migration Observatory briefing, COMPAS, University of Oxford, UK, February 2014.

Vygotsky, L.S. (1978). *Mind in Society: The development of higher psychological processes*. London: Harvard University Press

Wall, K. (2004). *Autism and Early Years*. London: Paul Chapman Publishing

Wall, K. (2006). *Special Needs and Early Years*, 2nd edn. London: Paul Chapman Publishing

Ward, J. (2012). *The Students Guide to Neuroscience*. Hove: Psychology Press

Warnock, M. and Norwich, B. (2010). *Special Educational Needs: A new look, 2nd edn*. London: Continuum International Publishing Group

White, J. (2010). *Two Year Olds Outdoors: Play, learning and development*. Siren Films Ltd.

White, R., Macleod, S., Jeffes, J. and Atkinson, M. (2010). *Local Authorities' Experiences of Improving Parental Confidence in the Special Educational Needs Process* (LGA Research Report). Slough: NFER

Whitty, G. (2002). *Making Sense of Education Policy*. London: Paul Chapman Publishing

Wise, L. and Glass, C. (2000). *Working with Hannah: A special girl in a mainstream school*. London: Routledge Falmer

Wolfendale, S. (ed.) (2000). *Meeting Special Educational Needs in the Early Years*. London: David Fulton Publishers

Wood, D., Bruner, J.S. and Ross, G. (1976). The role of tutoring in problem solving. *Journal of Child Psychology and Psychiatry,* 17: 89–100

Index

Abortion Act (1967) 11
access requirements 21
    people with disabilities, access to
        premises for 27–8
Acland Report (1908) 5
active learning 94, 96
adverse effects on outcomes,
    identification of 35
agencies not working together, dealing
    with difficulties of 29
Allen, Graham 40
Alliance for Inclusive Education
    (ALLFIE) 22
Anderson, Maggie 164
application for mainstream school (case
        study) 137
    Early Support Coordinator as guide
        through system 137
    Education, Health and Care Plan 137
    SEND Code of Practice 137
Approved Group Scheme 11
Area SENCOs (Special Educational
        Needs Coordinators),
        establishment of teams of 33
Armstrong, D. and Squires, G. 3
assess, plan, do, review cycle 43, 44–5,
        51, 52–3, 55, 72, 102, 159, 177–81
Association of Pre-school Playgroups 11
Audit Commission, report of (2002) 36–7

babies, communications of 143–4
Balfour Act (1902) 4
barriers to inclusion and learning,
    removal of 163
Basic Skills Agency 32
behaviour, development of 13
Bennathan, M. and Boxall, M. 115

Birsch, K.H. 10
Birth to Three Matters Framework
    (DfES, 2003) 34–5
    role of SENCO and 80
Boyle, C. and Topping, K. 4
brain development
    increasing awareness of 162
    role in learning ability and 12
British Association for Early Childhood
    Education 7, 41
British Council of Disabled People's
    Organisations (BCODP) 22

Care Standards Act (2000) 34
case studies xviii
    application for mainstream school 137
    characteristics of effective learning
        95–7
    child awareness process 73
    collaboration and responsive
        pathways to support 109–10
    common purpose, making it a daily
        reality 118–19
    coordination of support 128
    doing the best we can for each child
        61–2
    early identification and intervention
        54–5
    EYFS experiences 131, 132–3, 133, 134
    Family Partnership Model for
        outreach support 112–13
    finding an appropriate school 137–8
    first review meeting 88–9
    going to nursery school 78–9
    helping children and families 75–6
    inclusive approaches in primary
        school 115–16

keeping in touch 129
learning from parents 152
making our common purpose a daily
    reality 118–19
nursery school, participation at 154
parents' perspective 123–4
practitioner's perspective 108–9
preparation for a review meeting 85–6
progress from 13 to 25 months 98–100
review meeting at 12 months 91–3
SENCO role 57–8
special school, journey to 136–7
special school EYFS provision for
    children with ASD 148
starting at day nursery 69–70
transition to nursery school 67
transition to reception class in school
    124
transition to specialist provision 126
tuning into parents 60–1
understanding, looking to understand
    150
understanding child's needs 125
working together 129
working with an individual child;
    skills, strategies and approaches
    145–6
categorization 21–2
Census UK (2011) xii
Centre for Studies on Inclusive
    Education (CSIE) 156
child awareness process (case study) 73
    Development Matters (Early
        Education, 2012) 73
    early intervention strategies,
        conversations concerning impact
        of 73
    evidence and record keeping, linking
        different kinds of 73
    reviewing progress 73
    video observations 73
Child Care Act (2014) 164
child-centred approach following
    Plowden Report (1967) 12
Child Poverty Act (2010) 40
Children and Families Act (2014) xi, xiv,
    xvi
    child's perspective 142–3
    future prospects 158–9, 163
    legacy of Warnock Report and 42–3
    practitioner's perspective 108
    shared beginnings 3

Children and Young Persons Act (2008)
    38
Children's Act (1989) 23–4
Children's Act (2006) 156
Children's Commissioner for England
    164
children's needs, recognition and
    meeting of xii
child's perspective xvii, 142–57
    articulation of views, skill of 143
    babies, communications of 143–4
    case studies
        learning from parents 152
        nursery school, participation at
            154
        special school EYFS provision for
            children with ASD 148
        understanding, looking to
            understand 150
        working with an individual child;
            skills, strategies and approaches
            145–6
    Centre for Studies on Inclusive
        Education (CSIE) 156
    Children and Families Act (2014)
        142–3
    Children's Act (2006) 156
    common purpose, key person and
        144–56
        learning points 147, 149, 151, 153,
            155
        putting SEND Code into practice
            146, 148, 150, 152, 154
        things to think about 147, 149, 151,
            153, 155
        tuning into the child 145
    Council for Disabled Children 156
    Disability Rights UK 156
    Equality, Participation, Influence and
        Change (EPIC) 156
    improvement and development of
        practice 156
    inclusive approach, effective early
        years pedagogy and 143
    insight into, skills for gaining
        144–5
    key person, common purpose and
        144–56
        learning points 147, 149, 151, 153,
            155
        putting SEND Code into practice
            146, 148, 150, 152, 154

things to think about 147, 149, 151, 153, 155
tuning into the child 145
key points 157
learning from parents 152–3
learning points 153
putting SEND Code into practice 152
things to think about 153
Listening as a Way of Life (NCB Young Children's Voices Network, 2011) 156
London Borough of Ealing 156
Making Ourselves Heard (MOH) 156
National Children's Bureau (NCB) 143, 156
Northamptonshire Education 156
nursery school, participation at 154–5
learning points 155
putting SEND Code into practice 154
things to think about 155
Pre-school Learning Alliance 156
sensitivity of parents to babies' communications 143–4
special school EYFS provision for children with Autistic Spectrum Disorder (ASD) 148–9
learning points 149
putting SEND Code into practice 148
things to think about 149
themes 142
UN Convention on the Rights of the Child (Article 12.1) 142
understanding, looking to understand 150–1
learning points 151
putting SEND Code into practice 150
things to think about 151
Unique Child, concept of 143
Voice, Inclusion, Participation, Empowerment and Research (VIPER) 156
working with an individual child; skills, strategies and approaches 145–7
learning points 147
putting SEND Code into practice 146
things to think about 147
Young Children's Voices Network project 143, 156

Chronically Sick and Disabled Persons Act (1970) 15–16
Clark, A. 143, 156
Code of Practice *see* Special Educational Needs Code of Practice (DfE, 2014)
collaborative working 35–7, 77–80
collaboration between services, Warnock Report and 35–7
learning points 80
putting SEND Code into practice 79
things to think about 80
collaborative working (case study) 78–9
Early Support Development Journal 78
flexible and responsive support during transition to nursery school 78
shared knowledge and understanding, uses of 78–9
thinking beyond the setting 79
Common Assessment Framework (CAF) xvi, 36, 99, 165
common purpose 40–1
key person and 144–56
learning points 147, 149, 151, 153, 155
putting SEND Code into practice 146, 148, 150, 152, 154
things to think about 147, 149, 151, 153, 155
tuning into the child 145
common purpose as daily reality (case study) 118–19
Children and Families Act (2014) 119
collaborative working with parents 118
Educational Psychology Service 119
inclusion in maintained nursery school, approaches to 118
Key Person system 118–19
statutory assessment process 119
Unique Child, principle of 118
communication and language (CL) xv
development of 83–4
communication of purpose beyond special needs setting 59–63
improvement and development of practice 63
learning points 62–3
putting SEND Code into practice 62
communities of learners 31–2

comparison, collaboration and 23
competing priorities 107–8
Confucius xii
Contact a Family 50, 164
continuum of provision, idea of 163
contraceptive pill 11
Convention on the Rights of the Child
(UNICEF, 1990) 24
Cook, J. 84, 159
coordination of support (case study) 128
   communication between professionals
      128
   hospital, home and childminder,
      coordination between 128
Council for Disabled Children 78, 156
creativity, effective learning and 95
critical thinking, effective learning and
   95
cultural bias 22
Curriculum Guidance for the
   Foundation Stage (QCA 2000) 33,
   35

Davis, H. and Day, C. 122
day nurseries 14–15
day nursery, beginning at (case study)
   69–70
   building coherent links between home
      and setting 70
   favourite game, use of 70
   key person role during transition 69
   working together to make 'inclusion' a
      reality for all 69–70
day-to-day practice, continuation of
   91–4
   learning points 93
   putting SEND Code into practice 93
   things to think about 94
Department for Education and
   Employment (DfEE) 31–2
detrimental conditions 5
Development Matters (Early Education,
   2012)
   legacy of Warnock Report and 41
   Prime Areas of Learning and early
      identification of SEN 84
   role of the SENCO and 52
Dewey, John 12
disability
   awareness and understanding of
      10–11
   definition of 27

disability rights movement 22–3
disabled people, early educational
   provision for 4
real voices of people with disabilities,
   listening to 22–3
Disability Discrimination Act (1995) 27
Disability Rights UK 156
Disabled Persons (Employment) Act
   (1944) 9
Dyson, A. et al. 31

early education, purpose of 30–1
Early Help xvi, 99, 101, 165
early identification, Warnock Report
   perspective on 21–2
early identification and intervention
   (case study) 54–5
   communication between practitioner
      and SENCO 54
   interaction with new children and
      their families 54
   preparation for future multi-agency
      assessment 54
   specific aspects of SENCO role 55
early identification in early years
   provision 124–7
   learning points 127
   putting SEND Code into practice 126
   things to think about 127
Early Intervention: The next steps
   (Cabinet Office, 2011) 40
early intervention from birth 127–30
   learning points 130
   multi-agency involvement 128
   putting SEND Code into practice 130
   things to think about 130
Early Learning Goals (ELGs) 42
Early Support Programme (National
   Children's Bureau, 2013) 122–3
   pilot for 37
early twentieth century beginnings 4–10
The Early Years: Foundations for life,
   health and learning (DfE, 2011)
   39, 41
Early Years Action and Early Years
   Action Plus 34
Early Years Development and Childcare
   Partnerships (EYDCPs) 33
Early Years Foundation Stage (EYFS)
   xi, xii, xiii, xvi, xvii
   legacy of Warnock Report and 39
   framework for 35

Prime Areas of Learning xv
Principle into Practice cards 161
principled approach to xiv, xv, 65–82
Profile for (DfE, 2013) 42, 53
role of the SENCO, statutory
    framework for 49
special needs (SEN), early
    identification of xv
statutory framework xiv
see also EFYS provision, experiences
    of; principled approach to Early
    Years Foundation Stage (EYFS)
Early Years Outcomes (DfE, 2013) 52, 84
early years provision
    acceptance of positive impact of 31
    development of, shared beginnings
        and 11
Early Years Transition and Special
        Educational Needs (EYTSEN)
        Project xiv
Easton, C. et al. 108
education
    changes over time in provision of 107
    child at heart of educational process 8
    Education Action Zone 31–2
    Education for All movement 24
    human good of 20
    premises for, quality considerations
        for 5
    provision following from Warnock
        Report 27–8
    provision of 4
    system of, political influences on 4
Education, Health and Care Plan
        (EHCP) xvii, 40, 41, 43, 44, 58, 59,
        77, 130, 132
    legacy of Warnock Report and 43, 44
    multi-agency assessment leading to
        135–9
Education Act (1944) 9–10, 14
Education Act (1993) 27
Education Act (1998) 33
Education Act (2002) 34
Education Act (Schools) (1992) 27
Education (Handicapped Children) Act
        (1970) 16
Education Ministry, establishment of 9
Education Reform Act (1988) 23, 26
Educational Priority Areas (EPAs) 13
effective learning, characteristics of
        (case study) 95–7
    achievement, enjoyment of 96

active learning 96
choice of ways to do things 97
creativity 96–7
critical thinking 96–7
finding out and exploring 95
ideas and child having their own ideas
    96
involvement and concentration 96
making links 96
perseverance, keeping on trying 96
play and exploration 95
playing with what is known 95
understanding learning process 95–7
willingness to have a go 95
Equalities Act (2006) 37–8
Equalities Act (2010) 38, 163
Equality, Participation, Influence and
    Change (EPIC) 156
Evangelou, M. et al. 83
Evans, K. et al. 66
Every Child Matters (Green Paper,
    2003) 35–6
*Excellence for All Children: Meeting
    Special Educational Needs*
    (DfEE, 1997) 32
Excellence in Schools (White Paper,
    1997) 30, 34
experiences of EYFS (case study) 131
    academy attendance 133
    day nursery attendance 133
    day nursery support 132
    Early Years Inclusion Team, support
        from 132
    Education, Health and Care Plan 132
    Health Care Plan 132
    importance of child,
        acknowledgement of 132
    independent special school provision
        132–3
    Individual Education Plan 132
    Key Person approach 132
    local authority support 131
    nursery school attendance 133, 134
    nursery school support 132
    Portage, support from 132
    SEND Code of Practice 132
exploring, effective learning and 94
external services, involvement of
        98–101
    learning points 100
    putting SEND Code into practice 100
    things to think about 101

EYFS provision, experiences of 130–5
  learning points 135
  putting SEND Code into practice
    134–5
  things to think about 135
  Unique Child, concept of 131

Factory Act (1802) 4
Family Literacy initiative 31–2
Family Partnership Model
  characteristics of effective
    partnership 112
  parents' perspective 122
Family Partnership Model for
  outreach support (case study)
    112–13
  outreach support for children with
    SEN and disabilities 112
  responsiveness 113
Farrell, M. 3
Field, Frank 40
finding a school (case study) 137–8
  Children with Disability Team
    137–8
  fighting the system 137–8
  reporting inaccuracy, effects of 138
Forster Act (1870) 4
The Foundation Years (Cabinet Office,
  2010) 40
Froebel, Friedrich 5, 6, 7, 12
funding, allocation of 29
future prospects xvii, 158–66
  barriers to inclusion and learning,
    removal of 163
  brain development, increasing
    awareness of 162
  Child Care Act (2014) 164
  Children and Families Act (2014) 1
    58–9, 163
  Children's Commissioner for England
    164
  Contact a Family 164
  continuum of provision, idea of 163
  Equality Act (2010) 163
  EYFS (Principle into Practice cards)
    161
  include, desire to 162
  inclusive practice 158–9, 163
  individual influences on practice in
    EYFS 159–61
  National Award for SENCO
    qualification 159

parents as partners 161
*Parliamentary Inquiry into
  Childcare for Disabled Children*
  (2014) 164
Plowden Report (1967) 162
positives, identification of 161–2
professional relationships between
  colleagues, need for strength in
  159–60
relationships, bases for 160–1
respect for each other 161
Salamanca Statement on special
  needs education 163
SENCO, reflection on role of 159
SEND Code of Practice 158–9,
  164
  complementary nature of EYFS and
    163–4
Statement of Special Educational
  Needs 162
support for learning 161
themes 158
UN Convention on the Rights of the
  Child (1990) 163
Unique Child
  explicit focus on 158
  meeting needs through early
    intervention 159
'vulnerable learners' 165
Warnock Report 163
way forward? 161–6

Gaunt, C. 108, 165
genetics, role of 12–13
Geneva Declaration of the Rights of
  the Child (League of Nations,
  1924) 7
Gillard, D. 4, 8

Hadow Report (1931) 8
Hallett, F. and Hallet, G. 159
Harris, A. and Goodall, J. 74
Headstart programme (US) 31
Health Visitor Implementation Plan
  (2011) 38
Health Visitors, role of 22
Healthy Child Programme (2009) 38,
  41–2
Herbert, M. xii
historical perspective *see* shared
  beginnings
Hodge, Margaret 107, 164–5

improvement and development of practice
    child's perspective 156
    parents' perspective 140–1
    practitioner's perspective 121
    Prime Areas of Learning and early identification of SEN 102
    principled approach to Early Years Foundation Stage (EYFS) 81
inclusion
    barriers to inclusion and learning, removal of 163
    inclusive approach, effective early years pedagogy and 143
    inclusive attitudes, acquisition by practitioners of 51
    inclusive society, working towards 37–9
    integration of children with special needs, Warnock Report and 20
    international agenda on 26–7
    practice of, future prospects and encouragement for 158–9, 163
inclusive approaches in primary school (case study) 115–16
    annual targets 115
    behaviour recognition 115
    Boxall Profile 115
    City and Guilds 'Specialist Leaders of Behaviour and Attendance' course 115
    cohesive SEN provision 115
    impact of support 116
    Learning Zone (Year 1 upwards) 115
    staff training 115–16
    teaching assistant (TA) support 116
    Unique Child, concept of 116
inclusive community, creation of (case study) 160
    interactions, importance of 160
    opportunities, incidental conversations as 160
    positivity, importance of engagement and 160
Indicators of Education Systems (INES) 23
Individual Education Plans (IEPs) 34, 44
individual needs, striving to meet 56–9
    learning points 59
    putting SEND Code into practice 58–9

things to think about 59
    Warnock Report 23–4
individual needs of children, meeting with 71–4
    learning points 74
    putting SEND CODE into practice 74
    things to think about 74
Infant and Nursery Schools section of Plowden Report (1967) 12
information technology, use of 32
Intelligence Quotient (IQ) testing 13
internet, use of 32
Isaacs, Dr Susan 7, 8, 12

joint working 109

keeping in touch (case study) 129
    flexible communication 129
Key Person, common purpose and 144–56
    learning points 147, 149, 151, 153, 155
    putting SEND Code into practice 146, 148, 150, 152, 154
    things to think about 147, 149, 151, 153, 155
    tuning into the child 145
Key Person and learning from parents 152–3
    learning points 153
    putting SEND Code into practice 152
    things to think about 153
Key Person role 68–71
    learning points 71
    putting SEND Code into practice 70–1
    things to think about 71
key points
    child's perspective 157
    parents' perspective 141
    practitioner's perspective 121
    Prime Areas of Learning and early identification of SEN 102–3
    principled approach to Early Years Foundation Stage (EYFS) 81–2
    role of the SENCO 63–4
    shared beginnings 17
    Warnock Report 28
    Warnock Report, legacy of 45
Klein, Melanie 7
knowing the child, Key Person and SENCO collaboration 84–7
    background to child's story 85

extension of collaboration to include parents 84–5
learning points 87
putting SEND Code into practice 87
thinks to think about 87

labelling 21–2
learning from parents (case study) 152
Key Person, predictive skills of 152
listening and communication, connection between 152
parents and practitioners working together 152
signals from children 152
legislative process
shared beginnings 3–4
Warnock Report perspective 18
Life Long Learning Programme (2010) xii
Listening as a Way of Life (NCB Young Children's Voices Network, 2011) 156
literacy and numeracy, standards in 31
local authorities
educational responsibilities on basis of Education Act (1944) 9–10
provision for individual needs 23–4
services relating to children 36
London Borough of Ealing 156
looking to understand (case study) 150
hearing and understanding child's views 150
Key Person, experiences with 150
observation and understanding of communication, importance of 150
positive impact of child being listened to 150

MacKinnon, D. et al. 4
McMillan, Margaret 5, 7, 14
McMillan, Rachel 5, 7, 14
maintained nursery school 117–20
learning points 120
putting SEND Code into practice 119
things to think about 120
maintained primary school 114–17
learning points 117
putting SEND Code into practice 116
things to think about 117
Making Ourselves Heard (MOH) 156

The Marmot Review: Fair society, healthy lives (2010) 39
Mathers, S. et al. 163
Mental Deficiency Acts (1913-1938) 6
Mental Health Act (1959) 6–7
The Mind in Society (Vygotsky, L.S.) 12
monitoring 21, 28, 52, 53, 57, 65, 98–9, 149
performance monitoring targets 31
self-monitoring, concept of 25–6
Montessori, Maria 5, 7, 12
multi-agency assessment leading to Education, Health and Care Plans (EHCPs) 135–9
learning points 138
putting SEND Code into practice 138
things to think about 139
Munro, E. 162
Munro Report (2011) 39

'Named Person' 22
National Advisory Group on SEN (DfEE 1997) 32
National Autistic Society 113
National Award for SENCO qualification 159
National Care Standards Commission 34
National Children's Bureau (NCB) 11, 143, 156
National Curriculum, establishment of 31
National Foundation for Educational Research (NFER) 10
National Grid for Learning 32
National Health Service (NHS) 10
national statistics xii
Northamptonshire Education 156
Norwich, B. 3
Nurseries and Childminders Regulation Act (1948) 10
Nursery Education and Grant Maintained Schools Act (1996) 30
nursery school, participation at 154–5
learning points 155
putting SEND Code into practice 154
things to think about 155
nursery school, transition to (case study) 67
first experiences of nursery school 67

responding to parents' and children's current concerns 67

small steps, coming into the building and playing in the corridor 67

nursery school attendance (case study) 154

emotions, importance of listening in relation to 154

expectations, need for realism in 154

friendships, significance of encouragement in formation of 154

Key Person, experiences with 154

nursery school provision, beginnings of 14–16

nursery to primary school, transition from and to (case study) 61–2

common goal, aim of 62

empathy, need for 61–2

focus of discussions 62

Nutbrown, C. 7

Nutbrown, C., Clough, P. and Selbie, P. 3

Oates, J. et al. 94

observation

discussion and, importance of 101

observation-based planning process in EYFS 53

Office for Standards in Education (Ofsted) 27, 30

'one-to-one' support 81

open air activity 5

Opening Doors to a Learning Society (Labour Party, 1994) 30

Organisation for Economic Co-operation and Development (OECD) 23

outreach support 111–14

learning points 113

putting SEND Code into practice 113

things to think about 114

parents, collaboration and communication with 88–91, 101

learning points 90

putting SEND Code into practice 90

things to think about 91

parents' perspective xvi–xvii, 122–41

case studies 123–4

application for mainstream school 137

coordination of support 128

EYFS experiences 131, 132–3, 133, 134

finding an appropriate school 137–8

journey to special school 136–7

keeping in touch 129

transition to reception class in school 124

transition to specialist provision 126

understanding child's needs 125

working together 129

early identification in early years provision 124–7

learning points 127

putting SEND Code into practice 126

things to think about 127

early intervention from birth 127–30

learning points 130

multi-agency involvement 128

putting SEND Code into practice 130

things to think about 130

Early Support Programme (National Children's Bureau, 2013) 122–3

experiences of EYFS provision 130–5

learning points 135

putting SEND Code into practice 134–5

things to think about 135

Unique Child, concept of 131

facilitation of help for parents 123

Family Partnership Model 122

having a child with special needs 123

help for parents, facilitation of 123

improvement and development of practice 140–1

key points 141

multi-agency assessment leading to Education, Health and Care Plans 135–9

learning points 138

putting SEND Code into practice 138

things to think about 139

parents having children with special needs 123

personal advice to other parents in similar situations 139–40

positive relationships, principle of 123

skills for working with parents 122–3

themes 122

Parliamentary Inquiry into Childcare for Disabled Children (2014) 164
Pathfinder Champions 42–3
pathways to support (case study) 75–6
  Communication through Play (CTP) session 76
  possibility thinking 76
  'Stay and Play,' pathways from 75
  successful outcomes 76
Peel, Sir Robert 4
personal, social and emotional development (PSED) xv, 39, 115, 170–3, 175, 183
Personal Child Health Record (Red Book) xvi, 78
personal development 83–4
Pestalozzi, Johann Heinrich 5, 6, 12
physical development (PD) xv, 83–4
play plans, samples of
  assess, plan, do, review cycle and plans (blank and completed) for 4-year old diagnosed with ASD 177–88
  blank and completed plans for 2-year old 173–6
Plowden Report (1967) 11–14, 16–17, 162
  recommendations 17
Portage Home Visiting Service 20–1, 69, 129, 132, 133
positive relationships, importance of xi–xii, 108, 123
'possibility thinking,' confidence in xii, 76
poverty, impact on children's learning 30
practitioner's perspective xvi, 107–21
  case studies 108–9
    collaboration and responsive pathways to support 109–10
    Family Partnership Model for outreach support 112–13
    inclusive approaches in primary school 115–16
    making our common purpose a daily reality 118–19
  Children and Families Act (2014) 108
  competing priorities 107–8
  conversations with parents about accessing external support 108
  educational provision, changes over time in 107

engagement with services, helping families with 108
Family Partnership Model, characteristics of effective partnership 112
improvement and development of practice 121
joint working 109
key points 121
maintained nursery school 117–20
  learning points 120
  putting SEND Code into practice 119
  things to think about 120
maintained primary school 114–17
  learning points 117
  putting SEND Code into practice 116
  things to think about 117
outreach support 111–14
  learning points 113
  putting SEND Code into practice 113
  things to think about 114
positive relationships, principle of 108
practitioner knowledge about available support, importance of 108
SEND Code of Practice 108, 109
support, pathways to 109–11
  learning points 111
  putting SEND Code into practice 110–11
  things to think about 111
  themes 107
Pre-school Learning Alliance 11
Prime Areas of Learning and early identification of SEN xv, 83–103
  active learning 94
  case studies
    characteristics of effective learning 95–7
    first review meeting 88–9
    preparation for a review meeting 85–6
    progress from 13 to 25 months 98–100
    review meeting at 12 months 91–3
  communication and language development 83–4

concerns, highlighting of 101
creativity, effective learning and 95
critical thinking, effective learning
    and 95
day-to-day practice, continuation of
    91–4
    learning points 93
    putting SEND Code into practice
        93
    things to think about 94
Development Matters (Early
    Education, 2012) 84
early years development, factors
    particular to 83
Early Years Outcomes (DfE, 2013) 84
emotional development 83–4
exploring, effective learning and 94
external services, involvement of
    98–101
    learning points 100
    putting SEND Code into practice
        100
    things to think about 101
improvement and development of
    practice 102
interrelated nature of development
    areas 83–4
key points 102–3
knowing the child, key person and
    SENCO collaboration 84–7
    background to child's story 85
    extension of collaboration to
        include parents 84–5
    learning points 87
    putting SEND Code into practice
        87
    thinks to think about 87
observation, building pictures
    through 101
observation, discussion and,
    importance of 101
parents, collaboration and
    communication with 88–91, 101
    learning points 90
    putting SEND Code into practice 90
    things to think about 91
personal development 83–4
physical development 83–4
playing, effective learning and 94
rapid development 94–7
    effective learning, characteristics
        of 94–5

effective learning, use of
    characteristics of 95
    learning points 97
    putting SEND Code into practice 97
    things to think about 97
reflection on development progress
    101
social development 83–4
supervision, importance of process of
    84
themes 83
tracking sheets, examples of
    at 10 months old 170
    at 20 months old 171
    at 47 months old 172
principled approach to Early Years
    Foundation Stage (EYFS) xiv, xv,
    65–82
case studies
    child awareness process 73
    going to nursery school 78–9
    helping children and families 75–6
    starting at day nursery 69–70
    transition to nursery school 67
collaborative working 77–80
    learning points 80
    putting SEND Code into practice 79
    things to think about 80
improving and developing practice 81
individual needs of children, meeting
    with 71–4
    learning points 74
    putting SEND CODE into practice
        74
    things to think about 74
key person role 68–71
    learning points 71
    putting SEND Code into practice
        70–1
    things to think about 71
key points 81–2
support, pathways to 75–7
    learning points 77
    putting SEND Code into practice
        76
    things to think about 77
themes 65
Unique Child in context of EYFS
    65–8
    first impressions, importance of
        66
    learning points 68

putting SEND Code into practice 67–8
things to think about 68
private, voluntary and independent (PVI) sector 56
professional practice
  engagement with participants xi
  reflection on xi
  relationships between colleagues, need for strength in 159–60
provision, quality of xii, 9–10, 25–6, 32, 50–1
Pugh, G. and Duffy, B. 67

rapid development 94–7
  effective learning, characteristics of 94–5
  effective learning, use of characteristics of 95
  learning points 97
  putting SEND Code into practice 97
  things to think about 97
reflection *see* things to think about
responsible pedagogy, concept of 42
review meeting, continuing review of day-to-day practice (case study) 91–3
  communication and language needs 92
  Development Matters (Early Education, 2012) 92
  early identification of needs 91–3
  emotional development needs 92
  personal development needs 92
  physical development needs 92
  social development needs 92
  specialised advice, consideration about seeking 92–3
review meeting, monitoring progress (case study) 98–100
  coherent communication, provision of 98
  Common Assessment Framework (CAF) 99
  Disability Link Worker 98, 99, 100
  Healthy Child Programme 99
  Makaton sign language 99
  monitoring progress 98–9
  multi-agency involvement 99
  outcomes 99–100
  Personal Health Record 99

progress concerns, action agreements on 99
review meeting, preparation for (case study) 85–6
  'challenge' questions for clarification of thinking 85–6
  note-taking 86
  practical arrangements, suggestions for 86
  roles, talking through differences in 86
  supervision discussion 85–6
review meeting, progress review at first meeting (case study) 88–9
  communication and language 89
  Development Matters (Early Education, 2012) 89
  emotional development 89
  personal development 89
  physical activities, planning for 89
  physical development 89
  sensory experiences and coordinated movements 88
  social development 89
review meetings
  multi-professional meeting, prompt-sheet for 167–8
  sample invitation for 169
Rogers, B. and McPherson, E. 115
role of SENCO (case study) 57–8
  common understanding with parents, development of 57
  identification and responding to SEN 57
  local authority support 58
role of the SENCO 49–64
  assess, plan, do, review cycle 52–3, 72
  Birth to Three Matters Framework (DfES, 2003) 80
  case studies
    doing the best we can for each child 61–2
    early identification and intervention 54–5
    SENCO role 57–8
    tuning into parents 60–1
  communication of purpose beyond special needs setting 59–63
  improvement and development of practice 63
  learning points 62–3
  putting SEND Code into practice 62

Development Matters (Early Education, 2012) 52
domination by relationships with adults 80–1
Early Years Foundation Stage (EYFS), statutory framework 49
Early Years Foundation Stage Profile (DfE, 2013) 53
Early Years Outcomes (DfE, 2013) 52
facilitation of high quality provision 50
high quality provision, facilitation of 50
inclusive attitudes, acquisition by practitioners of 51
individual needs, striving to meet 56–9
   learning points 59
   putting SEND Code into practice 58–9
   things to think about 59
influence in establishment of support 50
Key Person approach 81
key points 63–4
observation-based planning process in EYFS 53
'one-to-one' support 81
'pack away' setting 56
parent carers, access to entitlements 50
private, voluntary and independent (PVI) sector 56
progress, addressing concerns about 72
provisional sufficiency 50–1
responsive and flexible approaches 81
SEND Code of Practice (DfE, 2014) 53
   need, identification of areas of 51–2
Special Educational Needs and Disability Discrimination Act (2001) 51
Special Educational Needs Code of Practice (DfE, 2014), role of the SENCO in 49–50
special educational needs coordinator (SENCO) 53–6
   learning points 55
   putting SEND Code into practice 55
   things to think about 56
support, analysis of needs 72

support, influence in establishment of 50
themes 49
tracking progress 51–2
transition, sensitivity to anxiousness of 61
Rousseau, Jean-Jacques 5, 12
Royal Commission on Lunacy and Mental Disorder (1926) 6
Rumbold Report (1990) 24, 25

Salamanca Statement on special needs education 26–7, 163
Sammons, P., Smees, R., Taggart, B., Sylva, K., Melhuish, E., Siraj-Blatchford, I. and Elliot, K. xiv
School Curriculum and Assessment Authority 31
self-monitoring, concept of 25–6
SENCO, reflection on role of 159
   see also role of SENCO
SEND Code of Practice (1994), tensions resulting from 32
SEND Code of Practice (2014) 42–3, 43–4
   complementary nature of EYFS and 163–4
   early years section, statements in 43–4
   future prospects 158–9, 164
   practitioner's perspective 108, 109
   role of the SENCO 51–2, 53
shared beginnings xiii, 3–17
   Abortion Act (1967) 11
   Acland Report (1908) 5
   Approved Group Scheme 11
   Association of Pre-school Playgroups 11
   Balfour Act (1902) 4
   behaviour, development of 13
   brain development, role in learning ability and 12
   British Association of Early Childhood Education 7
   child at heart of educational process 8
   child-centred approach following Plowden Report (1967) 12
   Children and Families Act (2014) 3
   Chronically Sick and Disabled Persons Act (1970) 15–16
   competition in international context, increased awareness of 4–6

contraceptive pill 11
'curriculum,' contents of 5
day nurseries 14–15
detrimental conditions 5
disability, awareness and
    understanding of 10–11
disabled, educational provision for 4
Disabled Persons (Employment) Act
    (1944) 9
early twentieth century 4–10
early years provision, development of
    11
Education Act (1944) 9–10, 14
Education (Handicapped Children)
    Act (1970) 16
Education Ministry, establishment of 9
educational premises, quality
    considerations for 5
Educational Priority Areas (EPAs) 13
educational provision 4
educational system, political
    influences on 4
employment-driven social mobility 14
environmental and hereditary factors,
    interactions of 13
Factory Act (1802) 4
Forster Act (1870) 4
genetics, role of 12–13
Geneva Declaration of the Rights of
    the Child (League of Nations,
    1924) 7
Hadow Report (1931) 7–8
    current thinking outlined in 8
'imperfect' home situations 5
individual differences between
    children, developing
    understanding of 8
Infant and Nursery Schools section of
    Plowden Report (1967) 12
infants, educational provision for 4
Intelligence Quotient (IQ) testing 13
key points 17
language development 13
legislative process 3–4
local authority educational
    responsibilities on basis of
    Education Act (1944) 9–10
'maladjustment' 13
medical advances 3
Mental Deficiency Acts (1913–1938) 6
Mental Health Act (1959) 6–7
mid-twentieth century 10–16

The Mind in Society (Vygotsky, L.S.)
    12
National Children's Bureau 11
National Foundation for Educational
    Research (NFER) 10
National Health Service (NHS) 10
Nurseries and Childminders
    Regulation Act (1948) 10
nursery school provision 14–16
open air activity 5
parental involvement 13–14
Plowden Report (1967) 11–14, 16–17
    recommendations of 17
political change 3
post-war priorities 9–10
Pre-school Learning Alliance 11
provision for children with special
    educational needs and disabilities
    9–10
relative academic performance 6
research, orientation of 6
Royal Commission on Lunacy and
    Mental Disorder (1926) 6
social mobility 14
societal change 3
special educational needs
    educational provision for 4
    Hadow Report reference to 8
Special Educational Needs Code of
    Practice (DfE, 2014) 3
specialist help, Plowden's recognition
    of need for 15
Summerfield Report (1968) 15
teachers, selection of 5–6
technological advances 3
thalidomide, impact of 10–11
themes 3
ultra-sound scans 11
Universal Declaration of Human
    Rights (UN, 1948) 10
war, influence of 6–7
Smith, R. et al. 163
Special Educational Needs and
    Disability Discrimination Act
    (2001) 33–4, 51
Special Educational Needs Code of
    Practice (2001) 33–4
    introduction of 27
Special Educational Needs Code of
    Practice (2014) xi, xv, xviii
    role of the SENCO in 49–50
    shared beginnings 3

special educational needs coordinator (SENCO) xiv, 53–6
learning points 55
putting SEND Code into practice 55
role of xiv–xv
things to think about 56
special school, transition to (case study) 136–7
Family Liaison Worker 136–7
independent special school 136–7
special school EYFS provision for children with ASD (case study) 148
communication of views about learning 148
home visits, value of 148
Key Person, experiences with 148
observation and understanding of communication, importance of 148
Starting with Quality (HMSO 1990) 24
Statement of Special Educational Needs process 32
future prospects 162
Steiner, Rudolf 7
Stewart, N. 94
Summerfield Report (1968) 15
supervision, importance of process of 84
support, collaboration and responsive pathways to (case study) 109–10
autism, provision for children with 110
diagnostic process (ASD) 110
health assessment and diagnosis process for ASD 109
pathways 109
Social Communication Difficulty Multi-Disciplinary Team (SCD), format of meeting 110
working together 109–10
support, pathways to
practitioner's perspective 109–11
learning points 111
putting SEND Code into practice 110–11
things to think about 111
principled approach to Early Years Foundation Stage (EYFS) 75–7
learning points 77
putting SEND Code into practice 76
things to think about 77

Support and Aspiration (Green Paper, 2011) 40–1
Sure Start xiv
Sylva, K. et al. 163

teachers, selection of 5–6
Team Around the Child (TAC) xvi, 126
technological advances 3
terminology, use of xvii–xviii
thalidomide, impact of 10–11
Thane, P. 9
themes
future prospects 158
parents' perspective 122
practitioner's perspective 107
Prime Areas of Learning and early identification of SEN 83
principled approach to Early Years Foundation Stage (EYFS) 65
role of the SENCO 49
shared beginnings 3
Warnock Report 18
Warnock Report, legacy of 29
Tickell, Dame Clare 39
Tickell Review (2011) 39, 41
tracking progress 51–2
tracking sheets, examples of
at 10 months old 170
at 20 months old 171
at 47 months old 172
transition to reception class in school (case study) 124
new relationships, establishment of 124
transition to specialist provision (case study) 126
Children's Centre sessions 126
Family Support Worker 126
links between EYFS provision 126
Team Around the Child (TAC) 126
tuning into parents (case study) 60
children, parents' established views of 60
long-term view, value of 60
working sensitively with parents 60

ultra-sound scans 11
understanding needs of child (case study) 125
family difficulties, effects of 125
parents' specialist knowledge, recognition of 125

social connections, support for 125
supervised contact visits 125
training courses and childcare
    qualifications 125
Union of the Physically Impaired
    Against Segregation (UPIAS) 22
Unique Child
    concept of xiv, xv, xvii
    in context of EYFS 65–8
        first impressions, importance of
            66
        learning points 68
        putting SEND Code into practice
            67–8
        things to think about 68
    explicit focus on, future prospects
        and 158
    meeting needs through early
        intervention 159
United Nations Children's Fund
    (UNICEF) 24
United Nations Convention on the Rights
    of the Child (1990) 43
    future prospects 163
United Nations Development
    Programme (UNDP) 24
United Nations Educational, Scientific
    and Cultural Organisation
    (UNESCO) 24, 26
United Nations Population Fund
    (UNFPA) 24
Universal Declaration of Human Rights
    (UN, 1948) 10

'vulnerable learners' 165
Vygotsky, L.S. 12

Ward, J. 94
Warnock, M. and Norwich, B. 135, 162
Warnock, Mary 166
Warnock Report xiii, 18–28
    access requirements 21
    access to premises for people with
        disabilities 27–8
    Alliance for Inclusive Education
        (ALLFIE) 22
    British Council of Disabled People's
        Organisations (BCODP) 22
    categorization 21–2
    Children's Act (1989) 23–4
    comparison, collaboration and 23
    consistency, coherence and 24

Convention on the Rights of the Child
    (UNICEF, 1990) 24
cultural bias 22
day care for 'children in need' 23
'deficit' view, moving on from 19
descriptive terms 21
disability, definition of 27
Disability Discrimination Act (1995)
    27
disability rights movement 22–3
early identification 21–2
early intervention 20–1
early years, focus on 25
education, human good of 20
education, purpose of 19–20
Education Act (1993) 27
Education Act (Schools) (1992) 27
Education for All movement 24
education provision following from
    27–8
Education Reform Act (1988) 23, 26
flexible working with young children,
    need for 25
'handicap,' outdated language of 20
Health Visitors, role of 22
inclusion, international agenda on
    26–7
inclusion, new thinking in moving
    towards 20
Indicators of Education Systems
    (INES) 23
individual needs 23–4
integration of children with special
    needs 20
key points 28
labelling 21–2
legislative process 18
local authority provision for
    individual needs 23–4
mainstream schools, extension of
    capacities of 20
monitoring 21
'Named Person' 22
Office for Standards in Education
    (Ofsted) 27
Organisation for Economic
    Co-operation and Development
    (OECD) 23
parents, practical and emotional
    issues for 22
play, need for planned and
    pleasurable play provision 25

Portage Home Visiting Service 20–1
purpose of education 19–20
quality improvements 25–6
real voices of people with disabilities,
    listening to 22–3
revolutionary aspects of 28
Rumbold Report (1990) 24, 25
Salamanca Statement on special
    needs education 26–7
self-monitoring, concept of 25–6
sensitivity 22
special educational needs, types of 21
Special Educational Needs Code of
    Practice, introduction of 27
special needs, assessment of 22
specialist provision, need for 22
Starting with Quality (HMSO 1990)
    24
sub-committees 19
themes 18
Union of the Physically Impaired
    Against Segregation (UPIAS) 22
United Nations Children's Fund
    (UNICEF) 24
United Nations Development
    Programme (UNDP) 24
United Nations Educational, Scientific
    and Cultural Organisation
    (UNESCO) 24, 26
United Nations Population Fund
    (UNFPA) 24
working groups 19
World Bank 24
World Conference on special needs
    education (UNESCO, Salamanca,
    1994) 26
World Wide Web, influence of 23
Warnock Report, legacy of xiii–xiv,
    29–45
adverse effects on children's
    outcomes, identification of 35
agencies not working together,
    dealing with difficulties of 29
Area SENCOs (Special Educational
    Needs Coordinators),
    establishment of teams of 33
assess, plan, do, review cycle 44–5
Audit Commission, report of (2002)
    36–7
Basic Skills Agency 32
Birth to Three Matters (DfES, 2003)
    34–5

British Association for Early
    Childhood Education 41
Care Standards Act (2000) 34
Child Poverty Act (2010) 40
Children and Families Act (2014)
    42–3
Children and Young Persons Act
    (2008) 38
collaboration between services 35–7
Common Assessment Framework
    (CAF) 36
common purpose 40–1
communities of learners 31–2
cross-agency focus on complexities of
    disadvantage 38–9
Curriculum Guidance for the
    Foundation Stage (QCA 2000) 33,
    35
Department for Education and
    Employment (DfEE) 31–2
Development Matters (2012) 41
differentiation and personalization,
    training in 31
earliness, how early is early? 34–5
early education, purpose of 30–1
Early Intervention: The next steps
    (Cabinet Office, 2011) 40
Early Learning Goals (ELGs) 42
Early Support Programme Pilot 37
*The Early Years: Foundations for life,
    health and learning* (DfE, 2011)
    39, 41
Early Years Action and Early Years
    Action Plus 34
Early Years Development and
    Childcare Partnerships (EYDCPs)
    33
Early Years Foundation Stage 39
    framework 35
Early Years Foundation Stage Profile
    (DfE, 2013) 42
early years provision, acceptance of
    positive impact of 31
Education Act (1998) 33
Education Act (2002) 34
Education Action Zones 31–2
Education Health and Care Plan
    (EHCP) 43, 44
Equalities Act (2006) 37–8
Equalities Act (2010) 38
Every Child Matters (Green Paper,
    2003) 35–6

Excellence for All Children: Meeting Special Educational Needs (DfEE, 1997) 32
Excellence in Schools (White Paper, 1997) 30, 34
Family Literacy initiative 31–2
The Foundation Years (Cabinet Office, 2010) 40
funding, allocation of 29
Headstart programme (US) 31
Health Visitor Implementation Plan (2011) 38
Healthy Child Programme (2009) 38, 41–2
inclusive society, working towards 37–9
Individual Education Plans (IEPs) 34, 44
information technology, use of 32
internet, use of 32
key points 45
literacy and numeracy, standards in 31
local authority services relating to children 36
local partnership working 33
The Marmot Review: Fair society, healthy lives (2010) 39
Munro Report (2011) 39
National Advisory Group on SEN (DfEE 1997) 32
National Care Standards Commission 34
National Curriculum, establishment of 31
National Grid for Learning 32
Nursery Education and Grant Maintained Schools Act (1996) 30
Office for Standards in Education (Ofsted) 30
Opening Doors to a Learning Society (Labour Party, 1994) 30
Pathfinder Champions 42–3
performance monitoring targets 31
personal, social and emotional development (PSED) 39
poverty, impact on children's learning 30

quality of provision, parents' views on 32
responsible pedagogy, concept of 42
revision of EYFS 41–2
School Curriculum and Assessment Authority 31
SEND Code of Practice (1994), tensions resulting from 32
SEND Code of Practice (DfE, 2014) 42–3
early years section, statements in 43–4
Special Educational Needs and Disability Act (SENDA, 2001) 33–4
Special Educational Needs Code of Practice (2001) 33–4
special educational needs in early years, support for 43–4
Statement of Special Educational Needs process 32
Support and Aspiration (Green Paper, 2011) 40–1
themes 29
Tickell Review (2011) 39, 41
UN Convention on the Rights of the Child 43
unemployment, impacts of 29
White, R. et al. 71
working together (case study) 129
accountability 129
collaborative working 129
evidence 129
motivation 129
positivity 129
working with an individual child, skills, strategies and approaches (case study) 145–6
emotions, responsiveness to 145–6
fun in learning process, importance of 146
moment-to-moment planning 146
sign and symbol communication system 146
World Bank 24
World Conference on special needs education (UNESCO, Salamanca, 1994) 26
World Wide Web, influence of 23